Ministry in an Oral Culture—Living with Will Rogers, Uncle Remus, and Minnie Pearl

*Ministry in an
Oral Culture—
Living with Will Rogers,
Uncle Remus,
and Minnie Pearl*

Tex Sample

WESTMINSTER/JOHN KNOX PRESS
Louisville, Kentucky

Scripture quotations from the New Revised Standard Version of the Bible are copyright © 1989 by the Division of Christian Education of the National Council of the Churches of Christ in the U.S.A., and are used by permission.

Book design by Susan E. Jackson

Cover design by Frederick N. Hagan II, Fearless Designs

First Edition

Published by Westminster/John Knox Press
Louisville, Kentucky

This book is printed on acid-free paper that meets the American National Standards Institute Z39.48 standard. ∞

PRINTED IN THE UNITED STATES OF AMERICA

9 8 7 6 5 4 3 2 1

Library of Congress Cataloging-in-Publication Data

Sample, Tex
    Ministry in an oral culture : living with Will Rogers, Uncle Remus, and Minnie Pearl / Tex Sample.
       p.   cm.
    Includes bibliographical references.
    ISBN 0-664-25506-x (alk. paper)
    1. Pastoral theology—United States. 2. Popular culture—United States. 3. Popular culture—Religious aspects—Christianity. 4. United States—Church history—20th century. I. Title. II. Title: Oral culture.
    BR526.S24   1994
    253—dc20   93-23713

To Peggy

795

Contents

Acknowledgments

I am indebted to a great many people who helped in the writing of this book. Many of the contributions are now lost to memory. While I hope that I have recorded in the notes or in the text itself the names of the many people who have assisted me, the acknowledgment of their help can never be complete.

Certainly I must mention Saint Paul School of Theology, its trustees, administration, staff, faculty, and students. It has been my privilege and honor to teach in such an open and free institution so singularly dedicated to preparing people for ministry in the church. In many institutions a person like me with my interests would have been out of place. The hospitality of Saint Paul for more than twenty-six years has made it home.

I am indebted to faculty colleagues and good friends with whom I have team taught in recent years while working out the notions and perspectives found herein: Kris Culp, Paul Jones, Kris Kvam, and Emilie Townes. Gene Lowry, a dear friend from the first day I arrived on campus, read the manuscript and helped me understand what I was trying to say. Larry Hollon teaches a course with me at Saint Paul that we call "White Soul: Country Music and the Working American." I have learned a great deal from him over the twenty years we have taught together.

Kathleen Campbell has worked with me as a research assistant for nearly a decade. Without her steady, reliable work, I simply could not get things done. Peggy Michael-Rush also served as my student assistant during the year that this book was written. I am grateful for her contributions throughout a long, hard twelve months.

This is the first book I have written on a computer. I have relied more than once on the help of Margaret Kohl, faculty secretary, in order to find my way through. I find that I am not "musical" when it comes to gadgets, especially technological ones.

This is the third book I have written with Harold Twiss as editor. I cannot thank him enough for his careful attention and sharp eye for confusion and potential miscommunication. I am greatly in his debt.

Finally, I met Peggy Sanford in the lunch room at Millsaps College in September 1954. Trying to impress her, I told all the funny stories and one-liners I knew, at least those that were presentable. Always generous of spirit, she laughed until she got indigestion. She has been my best friend ever since. We married in '57 and from that time on she has filled our home with beauty: music, art, drama, flowers, and, most beautiful of all, herself.

1

Will Rogers, Uncle Remus, and Minnie Pearl: Doing Ministry in a World of Stories

My first year of college was spent at Louisiana State University. I had gone there hoping to play baseball for the L.S.U. Tiger team, believing that I could soon get the attention of a scout and start pitching for the Yankees in but a few short years. I had everything it took to make it in the big leagues, well, . . . except for three things: I couldn't run, I couldn't hit, and I couldn't throw. But, except for those three things, I had it all.

That year turned out to be one of the most miserable years of my life. Not because of L.S.U.—which was a fine school—but because I was in the wrong place. I had fled from some mysterious "bump in the night" that kept telling me I had to go into the ministry. Going off to L.S.U. I had told God that I would major in "religious recreation." L.S.U., mind you, had no such program, but I figured I could just explain to God that my major in physical education was as close as I could come under the circumstances.

I learned that year that the call to go into the ministry is a lot like throwing up. You can put it off for a while . . . but there comes a time when you have *got* to do it.

So the next fall I went to Millsaps College, a fine Methodist liberal arts school in Jackson, Mississippi, where I should have gone to start with. The second day I was there I went to talk with my advisor. As we sat down, he said,

"Well, Tex, I see you are pre-ministerial."

1

"Yes, sir," I answered, trying to cover a flinch-jerk at his comment. I was not used to being called "pre-ministerial" and did not like it. You see, my daddy once told me that there were three kinds of people in the world with clean hands: people that don't work for a living, thieves, and preachers.

"And sometimes," he added, "you find all three in the same feller." Needless to say, I did not have a "high" view of ministry.

"Well," my advisor said, "I think you ought to take a course in philosophy."

"Oh, my," I answered with enthusiasm, "do you folks have a course on that here?"

"Of course. We have a *department* of philosophy."

I was quite simply thrilled. I had no idea such a thing would be taught there. All the way to the bookstore to pick up that $3.75 text I was jubilant. I couldn't wait. I was thrilled with the very idea that the college taught such a course, and that there was a book where someone had written down all the great lines of Will Rogers and Uncle Remus and Minnie Pearl. That all this would be available in one book that we would study throughout the fall semester filled me with excitement. This pre-ministerial stuff may be all right after all, I thought to myself.

Please understand, Daddy had told me many times growing up that Will Rogers was probably the greatest philosopher that ever lived, and I believed him. Of course, I knew about the great wisdom of Uncle Remus, and nobody got off better one-liners than Minnie Pearl at the Grand Ole Opry on Saturday night.

You cannot imagine my dismay when I later opened that book and started reading about some dumpy-looking little guy named "Sō-crat-is." (You may laugh at my pronunciation, but I did better than the boy from Louisiana who called him "Sō-crātes.") Socrates was talking about "tableness" and "chairness" and "ideas" and "truth, beauty, and goodness." My dreams for that fall semester crashed on the universalities of Socrates, and I grieved for the down-to-earth particularities of Rogers, Remus, and Pearl. It wasn't that Socrates didn't have any good lines. He said, "The unexamined life is not worth living," and I liked that, but I just had the feeling that he could have been so much better had he studied with Will Rogers.

Proverbs, Stories, and Relationships

You see, I had come out of an oral culture. My world was not one of discourse, systematic coherence, the consistent use of clear definitions, and the writing of discursive prose that could withstand the whipsaws of academic critique. Rather, it was a world made sense of through proverbs, stories, and relationships. A great deal of what we knew was tacitly understood: we often knew a lot that we could not put into words (because we didn't *have* the right words) but that we nevertheless knew how to *do*. We knew things we couldn't say, we felt things we couldn't name, and we did things we couldn't explain. So proverbs and stories helped us. They pointed to what we meant. No, actually, they *were* what we meant. If they lacked Socratic exactitude, they more than made up for it with color, hyperbole, metaphoric range, and their often earthy and concrete lack of polite taste.

First of all, then, an oral culture makes use of proverbs. Katie Cannon has said that "proverbs are short sayings made out of long experiences."[1]

Chinua Achebe reports that for the Ibo, a people in Central Africa, "proverbs are the palm oil with which words are eaten" and "the horse on which conversation rides."[2] In a discussion of Achebe's work, my colleague, Emilie Townes, suggests that a proverb can do any one or more of seven things:

1. explain human behavior,
2. serve as a guide for moral conduct,
3. explain social behavior,
4. serve to censure or criticize conduct,
5. give shrewd advice on how to deal with situations,
6. express egalitarian views,
7. express finer human qualities or emotions such as generosity.[3]

While Townes would not argue that these are exhaustive, they certainly make a helpful list. Proverbs were a basic teaching tool and a fundamental means for approaching life for the oral culture in which I was raised. At merely a hint of a suggestion they come tumbling from my memory. I was taught, "If it ain't broke, don't fix it" but we also knew that "the good is the enemy of the best." Hence, we were not raised without "tension" among these proverbs. They guided us in the appropriation of wisdom, one that came up against the hard edges of lives that often did not fit our fancy or come gently like a soaking night rain to end a drought.

The right proverb could mix humor with a dead-serious point about one's conduct. In our town we had a man who had come home from World War II shot directly in the *gluteus maximus*, not typically the site of a hero's wound. That would have been all right except that there was no end to his boasting about his courageous feats in combat. My father's cogent commentary took on proverbial status as the years went by: "Son, don't you ever come home from the war bragging like you won the Medal of Honor when you've been shot in the ass."

I am always looking for a statement of some kind that is universally true. My father, again, once said: "Son, them boards ain't gonna get up off the ground and nail themselves to that wall." You know, I have never once found an exception to that proverbial claim.

Second, an oral culture lives by storytelling. When there was a funeral in the family, we had a feast of stories. At Hartman's Funeral Home there was a coffee pot at the end of a hallway where the storytellers would gather during the wake and before the funeral. My uncles J. L., Paul, Elmo, and Junior, and my aunts Geneva, Virgie, Claudine, and Maxine would hold forth along with my uncles Bob White and Lavelle Biglane who had married Mama's sisters. They were magnificent. Sitting there on the floor I heard the oral tradition of the family. I learned there that a relative of mine—the meanest drunk, pound for pound, I ever knew and the sweetest person when she was sober—was once locked in a bedroom with nothing on but panties, bra, slip, and slippers because it seemed the only way to deal with her alcoholism. She went out the window in thirty-two degrees of Mississippi cold, hitchhiked 154 miles to New Orleans, and called home three weeks later to shout: "Whoooooah, I'm ready to come home!" I learned that when my uncle Paul was young, he could throw a hundred-pound sack of cement all the way over a flatbed rail car. And I discovered to my never-ending delight that the first time my mother ever saw my father take his clothes off, he was wearing red long-handles. My mother had reported later to my Aunt Virgie: "I have made a *mis*take."

Third, oral people think in relationships. It helps to understand relational thinking in contrast to that of a more abstract conceptual kind. I remember once taking an idea of mine about a stewardship campaign to my small traditional church. It was not a bad idea and, I thought, faithful to the way they did things there. After I explained it, however, no one said a thing. In my mind I imagined the idea as some small creature out there in the middle of the table writhing in stifled pain and dying. After an awkward and eternal silence I meekly suggested that we not consider it further at the present time and dropped it. At the next meeting of the board a month later, someone else raised the issue again, suggested it was a good idea, and asked me to get a few people to work on it. I was blown away! After the meeting I asked one of the trustees what on earth had happened. He said, "Oh, nothing really. It seemed like a good idea last month, but people needed to think about what it meant for everybody, you know, so nobody would be upset. We just needed to think how people in the church would be affected." Their initial silence had been because they had yet to work through the implications of the idea for the people of the church.

An issue that comes up will be considered in terms of the family and communal ties one has. A moral issue will be considered in the light of these same kinship and local connections. Any attempt at social change will need to be grounded in such relationships, and religious beliefs will be understood much more in relational than discursive ways. We will consider each of these cases later.

Traditional Orality

In the oral culture of my youth we knew how to read and write, but these skills were used basically to fill out forms at work, write checks or recipes, make lists of things to do, sign our names, read sports pages or romantic novels, take tests for driver's licenses, and, very occasionally, write letters or notes to friends and family. But the way we approached life—the way we celebrated things, the way we understood, the way we handled, mishandled, or avoided our feelings, hopes, or dreams—was oral. The best of our philosophers were not people who had written a shelf full of books; we were just not that "printy."[4] Our philosophers were people who knew exactly what to say: the fitting aphorism, the proverb that made people laugh or wince or growl or grunt in agreement, the conversation-ending thought for the day that said it all.

Of course, what was said was not always wise or humane. Sometimes it was hostile or racist or bigoted or sexist or self-serving or just plain wrong or all of the above. But such a position was not an expression of the genius of a traditional folk philosophy; it was a violation of it and an unfaithfulness to others who shared such understanding.

It is my contention that about half of the people in the United States are people who work primarily out of a *traditional orality*, by which I mean a people who can read and write—though some cannot—but whose appropriation and engagement with life is oral.[5] More than this, I am convinced that most churches have a clear majority of their membership who work from a traditional orality.

When one moves outside the United States into most of the rest of the world, the mass of oral cultures, both primary and traditional, looms even larger. Two-thirds of the people in the world are oral. To be "global in perspective"—if such a notion is anything more than a kind of pretentious dilettantism that only educated people could ladle on themselves—would require a much deeper appreciation of orality and oral culture.

Therefore, my basic interest here is to look at the traditional orality of our culture to suggest ways that literate clergy and laity may become far more appreciative of and adept at working with people who face life and death, personal and social relationships, morality and faith, and God and the world with a traditional orality.

Those of us who have been to the university and the seminary are not only unequipped, usually, to work within these settings, we typically do not even like such people. We often characterize their folk wisdom with words like "cliché" or "bromide." We see their tastes as bucolic, as redneck, as primitive, as illiterate, as unsophisticated, as lacking in urbanity or education or polish or all of the above. We view them as people who are not capable of critical, informed thinking. They are "common" or "average" we say, when we really mean vulgar, and this in its pejorative sense.

In asserting this I am not talking only about the responses of conservatives and reactionaries. In my experience most left-wingers—my own political position—don't give a damn about such folks except perhaps as some hoped-for vehicle of change or as casebook evidence for the failure of the U.S. capitalistic system. They don't mind fighting for justice for such people, but, please, don't make them have to associate with these lowbrows. And some clergy! I talked recently with a pastor starting a new church in a large suburban area. When I told him that a large number of working people (who are mostly oral) lived in the area, he told me flatly that he really had no interest in them. He wanted a first class church made up of top business and professional people, the kind with whom he could work. He may perhaps have the opportunity to continue that ministry in hell, although, of course, I don't make those decisions.

Let me be clear, too, that I am not talking only about Anglo-European whites. The powerful place of a traditional orality among African Americans, Hispanics, Native Americans, and Asians in United States society must not be forgotten. Indeed, part of the genius of the black church has been the continuity of its oral practices in preaching, worship, and other dimensions of congregational life.[6] Henry H. Mitchell and Nicholas Cooper-Lewter speak directly to this issue in their discussion of "soul theology" and the place of oral tradition in its practice.[7]

Hispanics in the United States also come from profoundly important oral traditions. One book reports the conversation of Hispanic women discussing their understanding of God. The account is a moving example of an oral tradition and its rich, culturally specific metaphors for talk of God and faith. One of the women, Inez, described God as a

> *sentimiento* [a deep feeling], a force that makes me move, which pushes me in difficult moments . . . something I cannot explain. But if they would ask me to draw God, I would draw my grandmother

smiling. Because she is the only person that I believe has filled me or filled me so much that I can compare her to God.[8]

Oral traditions are also inextricably a part of the enormous diversity of Native American life in the United States. Through their oral histories "pictures" of the past are handed down. The Sioux are a good example.

> To begin their tribal history . . . many of the Sioux went back to the beginning of time when Wakan Tanka (The Great Spirit) was walking through the Black Hills of South Dakota. Surveying the fruits of his creations, he was pleased. He gloried in the gifts he had given to the animals: strength to the bear, swiftness to the hawk, grace to the deer, perseverance to the turtle, and majesty to the eagle. He had but one more gift to impart, and that was love; so Wakan Tanka joined with the Earth Mother and created the first man right there in the Black Hills. This story was the very fabric of Sioux life.[9]

This is no place even to attempt to broach the inex-haustible—in human terms—range of human life and history in Asian traditions. Perhaps an illustrative hint of the importance of traditional orality can be found in contemporary Korean *Minjung* theology. *Minjung* is a word that cannot be defined because it is not a concept. It can only be symbolized as the reality of the way life is for Korean people "because of its characteristics of unmediated knowledge and the transparency of experience." It is "a living religious symbol in which people can participate and with which they can identify." The spirit of *Minjung* is *han*, another untranslatable word, and a word that can only be approached through stories and is not a concept. "We must listen to the *story* of *han*. *Han* may not unfold itself without the telling of stories." These stories are the *Mindam* (the folklore), "the house in which the spirit of the *Minjung* dwells." *Han* can be known in the traditional stories, in dance, opera, native songs, and in the true stories of oppressed Korean people.[10]

In thinking of Hispanics and Asians one moves inevitably beyond the United States to a world where mammoth numbers of people live in oral cultures and traditions. The challenge to learn the skills of orality has staggering implications for ministry.

I cannot help but wonder what might happen if Christian evangelism and prophetic ministry took form in oral expression and in faithful folk theologies. Except for a vital and living trust in, and obedience to, God, nothing is more important than the formation of native Christian communities that can address the personal and social captivities, the existential and historical illusions, and the lethal principalities and powers of our time.

As I work through this book, my focus will be basically on orality among more traditional Anglo-European people. I hope this will not be seen as ethnocentric arrogance, but as humility before the mystery of other traditions. I will, of course, report from time to time insights from African Americans, Asians, Hispanics, and Native Americans, and from peasant and more primal cultures, but I think this is not the time for white people (like me) to be "telling about" other people. I do dare to wish that these comments may open conversations with those in other traditions about the importance of orality and its implications for our lives together.

Therefore, in the next chapter, I want to look briefly, and only in a suggestive way, at what indigenous ministry would look like if it were done in terms of a traditional orality instead of a literate style.

I know of no better place to begin a discussion of traditional orality than with Walter J. Ong's wonderful book *Orality and Literacy*. His discussion focuses on the differences between oral and literate cultures, but he makes an important distinction between *primary oral cultures* and *secondary oral cultures*.[11] The former is a culture without a written language, and the latter a culture with a written language that also has a *residual oral culture* operating within it. It is this latter type I am interested in and will focus on throughout this book.

Let me say, too, that I find Ong's characterization of a secondary oral culture as *residual* to be an unfortunate use of language. To describe the oral culture of perhaps half the people in the United States as "residual" significantly distorts their lives. Ong seems to be operating with a kind of developmental understanding that sees orality passing from history and present now only in these residual locations, dying but hanging on for the time being. My suspicion is that orality is a significant way simply to

engage life and will be with us into any foreseeable future, provided one does not see orality as ahistorical. Orality is profoundly complex and changeable. It cannot be reduced to one
abstract form. More than this, to depict the concrete lived lives of
people who manage to survive and cope—often being poor and
near poor—and who do so with an endurance that would wilt
and outpace most "literate" people I know, and then to call their
culture "residual," is not only demeaning, it names something a
"leftover," a "remains," a "leavings," that, in fact, has as much
permanence as writing itself. There is *no* literate culture without
this "residual" orality. Therefore, I will refer to oral practice in a
literate culture as "traditional orality" in order to avoid some of
the unfortunate connotations of calling it "residual."

Still, though, someone may press further and argue that
both oral and literate cultures are being surpassed by an electronic orality. With the coming of the telegraph, the telephone,
the radio, the television, the computer, and the growing electronic formatting of media, some maintain that a visual and oral
organization of communication is occurring on a worldwide
scale that will sweep everything before it in the twenty-first century. Some believe such electronic orality will not only transform
literacy but will destroy traditional orality.

Barry Tedford is my next-door neighbor, a man from
Bruce, Mississippi, who worked for a good many years as the
yard foreman in a hardwood lumber company. I often consult
Barry about popular culture because he has a good intuitive
sense of things. For example, I recently asked him about the
"meaning" of a pickup truck, and he gave me the best disserta-
tion on that mechanical and symbolic marvel I have read, heard,
or seen *anywhere*. For example, he told me that in a pickup truck
you can spit down on the top of *any* car—Mercedes, Cadillac,
BMW, you name it—and you know, you can! I asked him also
about what was happening to storytelling and "really good sayings."

"Well, Tex, it's changing," Barry said. "People don't sit
around anymore like they used to on the porch of a store or
down at the fire station or out in the backyard and tell stories
and carry on the way we used to. Television is killin' it. People
stay home and sit around and watch TV."

As we talked, however, we both realized that we, in fact, had been sitting there for an hour telling stories and "getting off one-liners." We laughed at the irony of practicing traditional orality to pronounce its demise. The requiem was sung by the "deceased."

My point is not that electronic orality is unreal. It is here and powerfully so. But also present is the literate culture on which electronic orality is based, and so is the oral culture. For example, I follow country music with some interest. It is obviously based in great part in electronic media. One does not have to listen very long, however, to realize how deeply influenced it is by proverb and story, by tacit understanding, and by folk wisdom. Garth Brooks sings a song with a great title—"Friends in Low Places."[12] Ray Stevens tells us the story about the Mississippi Squirrel Revival at the First Self-Righteous Church of Pascagoula,[13] and Kathy Mattea exhorts us in one of her songs that our living, our singing, our loving, and our dancing have to "come from the heart."[14]

Moreover, if there ever was an instance of oral culture influencing electronic media, rap is it. Walter Ong outlines the many ways in which oral culture depends on memory and the importance of memorization. Rap is clearly an oral practice that the music industry has taken on because of its wide appeal and, hence, commercial success. But country music and rap are only two illustrations of a wide range of practices carried out in popular culture that have been gathered up for their appeal to large numbers of people in the society. The presence of oral practices in easy-listening, rock, jazz, and blues, for example, cannot be ignored. The soap operas on TV are virtual photocopies of oral storytelling with their "heavy" ceremonial characters, their stereotyped and/or formulaic expressions, their standardized themes, their cultivation of praise and blame, and their copious treatment of a subject. These are all characteristics of oral culture helpfully discussed, again, by Ong.

Ours is not a future of electronic orality devoid of literality and traditional orality. Instead, it is one where all three will be with us into any projectable time to come. What this bodes for the church is ministry that can be sensitively indigenous. We need forms of ministry that can call forth from clergy and laity and from congregations and denominations the capacity to worship, proclaim, teach, and witness in expressions that are authentic to the lives of the diverse peoples of the United States. It could hardly be a more exciting challenge. We are offered an opportunity to be local on a road that is not parochial and to be "global" on a thoroughfare that is not abstract. Let us turn, then, to some characteristics of traditional orality that will help us reconsider the style of the church's ministry and mission.

2

The Practices of Traditional Orality: Doing Ministry with Traditional/Oral People

Let me begin then with a truism. What you cannot remember in an oral culture you do not know.[1] As simplistic as this sounds, it has significant import for traditional orality and for the life of the church. In oral cultures there are no books, no manuals, and no reference works. If one is not able to recall something, one simply will not know it. In the traditional orality of our own society, entire territories of a person's life are dependent on memory, not texts, and these persons find themselves in a very different place from those who went to the university or the seminary.

Knowledge, Memory, and Recall

Kris Culp, the Dean of the Disciple House at the University of Chicago and a very literate person, once taught theology as a colleague for six years at Saint Paul. While in Kansas City she bought a nice bungalow on Cherry Street. She wanted to plant several flower beds around the place, and while she had received some training about such things from her mother when she grew up, Kris nevertheless wanted to do it very well, the way she does just about everything. So she bought this tome of a book on raising flowers. She read it in detail. She became so good with flowers that I now believe she could stick a piece of aluminum in the ground, and it would bloom. (Note that hyperbole is basic to orality!) This is a literate way to learn about flowers.

A contrasting story has to do with the time when our church schools began to move away from the memorization of Bible verses. Perhaps such memorization was considered authoritarian or too biblicist or lacking in subtlety or not sufficiently appreciative of the context of scripture or perhaps just poor teaching method or whatever. I remember that I, as a fresh-faced twenty-five-year-old seminary graduate, wanted the children and youth to be taught a more sophisticated approach to scripture so that when they grew up they would not have to throw off the kind of literal interpretation I had grown up with.

So I went to the next board meeting and announced that we were no longer going to teach children to memorize scripture verses, but instead we were going to "explain what they meant" (which in the light of contemporary literary criticism is no small feat). I argued that if the children knew what the verses meant, it would not matter whether they could quote them. I had hardly started when I was interrupted by Margaret Jones, one of the matriarchs of that church, a truly sweet person, and one of my strong supporters.

She said: "Tex, we're not going to do that."

"But, Margaret, this is now being recommended by leading experts in the church."

"I don't care. We are not going to do that."

"Margaret, can't you say *why*?" I asked with some frustration. "I'm trying to give leadership here," I said to myself.

"Look, Tex, we love you," she said compassionately, perhaps to relieve some of the obvious hurt on my face, "but you need to understand. Most of our children drop out of church when they are fourteen, fifteen, or sixteen. Then they graduate or 'quituate' from high school, work in one of the shoe factories here in town, marry, and eventually have kids of their own. Our hope is that when those kids get four or five years old, our young people will bring them back to church. But from the time they leave this church until, we hope, they return, the only Bible they will have is the one in their heads. That's why we are going to teach them to memorize Bible verses. If it's in there [in their minds and memories], someday they may come back to the church because they learned early how important faith is."

The point here is that traditional orality has requirements

for Christian education and life in the church quite different from those of a more literate cast, although all of us may learn from the wisdom of traditional orality.

I think particularly of those times in the history of the church when the catechism was used, in part, because many people were not literate and such memorization provided the means for a clear expression of the faith against corrosive and less authentic expressions of the Christian story. Today, memorized verses from the hymnody are often the most sharply articulated statement of the faith many people have, a tribute to the importance of the hymns—especially to those for whom a more discursive statement is foreign to their lives.

Christian educators like Dick Murray are instructing us again on the importance of memorization of scripture for children. Dick tells the story of being in a foxhole in combat during World War II. Fearing for his very life, he began to quote to himself all the scripture he knew. He would agree with Margaret Jones about how important it is that children have scripture "in their heads."

I remember what I used to hate about the memorization of Bible verses. The teachers always started on the other side of the room with Linda Becker, who was very smart. By the time they got to me, all the well-known verses had been used, especially, "Jesus wept," and I wound up being embarrassed. Dick has a way around this. He suggests that the children memorize the verses, but then quote them as a group together. Not only does this alleviate the problem I had but also it communicates something very positive about the corporate nature of the church.[2]

Memorization is, of course, very important in worship. In many settings and with a large number of people, the liturgy needs to be more oral, less "printy," and to make more use of practices like chant and response. In many settings, use of the bulletin with the conventional twelve to fourteen items could be mercifully done away with for people who are traditionally oral and especially for those who are functionally illiterate. Obviously, this suggestion is not appropriate for more literate congregations, but it would be a godsend for many in this society who see highly literate services as a subtle, or not-so-subtle exclusion of who they are. The point here about memorization is that it takes on increasing importance in such services. One pastor who realized that all of his congregation was traditionally oral—in my terms—changed the service. Many of them had memorized the Twenty-third Psalm, or most of it, early in life. He decided to use this as a confession of faith. In other parts of the service he would, for example, line out well-known scriptures or creeds until they were known by the congregation. Such worship over the course of his ministry developed affirmations of faith, scripture verses, and the lyrics of hymns. They built a memorized "text."

The return to a greater use of memorization, really a reconsideration and a restructuring of the congregational life of churches with traditionally oral people, can indeed turn liturgy into the work of the people. Such sensitivity and indigenousness can communicate to millions of people in this society a word made "flesh" that truly "dwells" with us.

Learning By Apprenticeship

When Peggy and I left Millsaps College for me to go to seminary at Boston University, we found the Northeast to be radically different from our Mississippi roots. I remember going to the largest supermarket in the area to ask if they had grits. The clerk told me I would have to go to a hardware store!

We greatly missed the local food of Mississippi. We particularly missed those magnificent icebox rolls that Peggy's mother made. They were the kind of rolls you had to chew real fast before they simply melted in your mouth.

One night in Boston I told Peggy how much I loved her mother's icebox rolls and how much I missed them.

"Well, why don't we call her and ask for the recipe?"

"Oh, do you suppose she would let us have it?" I asked, sensitive to the fact that sometimes recipes are like mystery religions and their possessors guard them closely.

"Well, let's try," Peggy said.

When we called, her mother seemed genuinely touched by our appreciation for her culinary art and indicated she would send the recipe the next day. When it arrived, it said this:

Pour some flour in the bottom of a bowl
Put in a dash of baking soda
Add a pinch of salt.
Pour in some milk.
Stir it until it looks right
Bake it to a honey brown.

Stymied, we called her on the phone again. "We are thrilled to get the recipe," I said, trying to sound as appreciative as I really was, but also not wanting to be affrontive about the fact that the unspecific nature of her recipe was not adequately helpful. "We do have a few questions," I went on. "You say, 'put some flour in the bottom of a bowl.' Uh, how much flour?"

"Well, it depends on how many rolls you want to make," she answered with more than a hint of frustration.

"I see . . . okay . . . uh, how much . . . is . . . a . . . *dash*?"

"Well," she said, moving from frustration toward exasperation, "a dash is a dash. *Everybody* knows what a dash is."

"Of course," I answered, now attempting to placate her and wondering how and why I ever got myself into this spot with my mother-in-law of less than a year. Trying now to appear as less than the bumbling ignoramus I felt myself to be, I tried covering my over-exposure with the weak line: "*and a pinch is a pinch.*"

"What else would it be?" she said, with a sense for the reality of things that at that moment seemed to have evaded *me* all my life.

"Look, Tex, this isn't working," she said as she put an end to this ritualized blood-letting of my dignity. "You wait until you two come home this summer, and I will take you into my kitchen. Then, I'll *show* you how to make icebox rolls."

That following summer, as she apprenticed us on the making of icebox rolls, I realized that she could never have conveyed her art to us through the literal framework of a recipe. Too many things were going on for her to capture them on a written page.

I learned then that traditional/oral people do not learn by "study," but through apprenticeship. Walter Ong defines study as "sequential, classificatory examination," a process that is impossible without writing, and he argues that primary oral cultures do not study.[3] To study, one writes down key ideas, definitions, and concepts, and then compares and contrasts what was said in one place with what was said in another. This, in an attempt to be as clear and exact as possible. This is study.

Peggy's mother did not study. Oh, of course, she did do some study, but this was not her basic way to learn. Like traditional/oral people, she learned and she taught by apprenticeship. I remember that she once took a college course in religious studies. Always very bright, she did well in the course, but I remember how much she talked about the difficulty of the work—reading of the text and putting concrete reality to the ideas. As highly motivated as she was, the process was simply alien to her.

My guesstimate is that half the people in the churches are like this. It may be that, in regard to their lives in the church, the percentage is even higher because many people were raised in the church, and an oral approach to things religious was set early and remains so.

Considerations like these have led me to ask questions about the literate cast of a good deal of church programming. If young people and adults are basically oral in their approach to life, and they continually find themselves in churches that are literate, these folk will not likely continue to come. As anyone who knows much about the church understands, many people who will come to church when there is something to do—paint a room, rebuild a wall, cook a supper, provide volunteer time for a community service—will not come to a Sunday school class or to worship. I have always been struck by the number of youth who will come to Scouts, with its strong apprenticeship and merit badge approach, but who will not come to Sunday school. Moreover, most of the adult Sunday school classes that are really effective with people out of the lower 60 percent of the class structure are far more likely to be communal gatherings with a wide range of practices, socials, and service projects for the group than "classes" for study as such. Please understand, I am certainly not opposed to, but rather actively support, people who want to study the faith and mission of the church. My point, instead, is that this is not indigenous to the lives of a majority of people in the United States.

For these reasons I think a significant part of the ministry and mission of our churches needs to be done in an apprentice-ship way. The Sunday school needs options that are oriented around learning from church members while carrying out the ministry and mission of the church. Certainly a part of the ge-nius of the black church in the United States has been its highly differentiated structure and its many roles and jobs. This charac-teristic opened a range of options where others could learn by assisting the more experienced people in the church.

For traditional/oral people much is to be learned in the teaching that occurs through hands-on mission. For example, Habitat for Humanity is a significant program because its mis-sion clearly has a theological and faith purpose and meaning, and because for a good many, participation involves learning on the job. So much of our work in the church involves teaching people *about* the faith and *then* asking how this can be imple-mented. Certainly an enormous opportunity awaits those who learn in apprenticeship roles where faith issues arise and need to be addressed in the active work of discipleship.

Concrete Life-Based versus Introspection

One of the classes I taught at Saint Paul School of Theology had as its project the assignment to interview "hard-living" peo-ple at homeless shelters, detox centers, urban ministry settings, bars, honky-tonks, and a few private residences. We wanted to focus on people who tended to abuse alcohol and other drugs; who had a history with violence either as perpetrator, victim, or both; who had struggled with household and/or family relation-ships; who were politically alienated; who often had jail records; and who were living in poverty or near to it.[4]

Early on in the work one of our students who was very able, who had finished a lengthy course in clinical pastoral edu-cation, and who was sensitive and related well with people, came back to class with a serious complaint. Her interview had not worked! She reported that the people she talked with would tell her a terribly painful story in answer to an interview ques-tion. Having been well trained to help people deal with their feelings, she would respond to some deeply hurtful experience reported by her interviewee by saying things like this: "What did that feel like?"; "How did you feel about that?"; or "That must have *felt* awful." In class that day she reported: "It just stops the conversation."

Others in the class also indicated that the interview questions did not seem to work well. The hard-living people simply were not comfortable with our questions. They were not getting at any real issues.

In session that day we started to talk through the problems students had encountered and, in the process, dropped the whole idea of a questionnaire or even a structured interview. We decided, instead, to engage the people in the telling of their personal life stories. We did have some concerns we wanted to ask about if they did not come up "naturally," but we would basically focus on their stories. We were pleased to discover that those being interviewed responded well to this approach. When they came to a really hard time, we did not ask them how they felt, or other kinds of questions designed to elicit their subjective feelings, but instead stayed with a story-line approach. Our response changed from "How did you feel about that?" to questions like "What did you do?" or "What happened next?" or "How did you get through that?" Such questions kept the *story* going. We *did* learn a great deal about feelings, from the contents of their stories—more than we had by delving into their subjective feelings alone. It was a very effective approach.

What was going on here? An insight of Walter Ong's made a great deal of sense in understanding what we had experienced. Ong makes the important point that the focus on interiorization and introspection emerges with writing and print cultures. These literate societies, he contends, enable people to examine feelings and thoughts in the deep interiors of subjective life. He sees print cultures as providing the opportunity for the emergence of a "privatized, interior shift in religion," for the search for the obscurities and deeper meanings of depth psychology, and for a more privatized culture as seen in the shift to the nuclear family. But most of the hard-living people were oral in the traditional sense. Of course, some of them were introspective and focused on their own subjectivity, but this was not typical. They dealt with their concerns in a far more concrete, life-based sense that made its more articulate expressions in story.[5]

During that same period of time I was able to get a transcription of a wonderful sermon by a Pentecostal African-American preacher in which he dealt with the New Testament story of the man who had lain by the pool for thirty-eight years because no one would help him, but crowded him out when the water was troubled. The preacher had asked what was going on "inside the man." I was immediately interested to see what he would say. How would he deal with the man's intrapsychic feelings? Would he focus psychologically on his subjective experience? Would he do some careful, probing analysis of his interior state? If so, how would he communicate it to a congregation that was clearly oral?

His answer was strikingly on the money with Ong's insight. At the crucial turn in the sermon the pastor "explained" what was wrong with the man: *"He was lying down in his mind. Until he could stand up in his mind,* he could not get up and help himself."

The more I have contemplated these and related experiences, the more convinced I am that the psychological cast of so much of the church's work (with its focus on the interiors of people), has distanced us all the more from people whose orality gives them more concrete, life-based concerns. Just think about the pervasive psychological perspectives, methods, procedures, and skills that have been used by clergy and laity in the church that involve a focus on the interiority of people's lives: transactional analysis, Gestalt therapy, reality therapy, Jungian psychology, Meyers-Briggs personality types, Freudian object-relations theory, family systems theory, Rogerian non-directive counseling, as well as all the stage theories based around maturity, morality, and faith that tend to associate higher development with literate people. Or, what can be said about the psycho-technic skills of communication with their repertoires for analyzing defensive, rationalizing, passive-aggressive, reactive, threatening, projecting, co-dependent, dysfunctional, blaming—and so on—behavior? One can doubtlessly find any of these to be helpful, and still see why oral people would experience this as an unpentecostal glossolalia. Moreover, one would not have to take a know-nothing position or be unappreciative of the gifts of psychology and other behavioral sciences to maintain that the church might just be a whole lot better if it privileged the gospel and the language of its own scripture and tradition. Like any other discipline, the human and social sciences can be imperious and colonial. Oral people—had they the words and the training to accompany their smarts—could make this case in terms of their "exile" in a church devoted, even unintentionally, to those who are decidedly not them.

Now let me turn the matter in a constructive direction. The point is not that the church should now become oral only in its approach and throw the literate sophisticates out head-first on their highbrow faces. No, while the uncritical literate life is shamanism reduced to its lowest form, it can also be a beautiful expression of loving God with all one's mind. All literates are not Philistines and pagans, although those blinded by their individualism, drunk on their "autonomous reason," hooked on the nation-state, sold out to fat-cat wealth, and acting the prodigal knower on an Archimedean veranda, clearly seem to qualify.

Obviously, a church that has a ministry and mission in this world will need to be literate. It will, also, need to be oral. This means finding the way to be concretely life-based with people who may very well make up the majority of its members, and the majority of the unchurched as well.

What would this look like? There is a sense in which this entire book aims to do that, but for now let me suggest that many mainline churches need to reexamine traditional *practices*, especially those characteristic of oral people. It is no secret that people in the lower half of the class structure are more likely to have family devotions, say grace at meals, attend worship, and participate in other such actions. Their lives are lived out more in traditions and practices than they are in thinking and knowing the faith. They are, for example, much more likely to do devotions than to do seminars. If up-scale Protestants tend to be the Republican Party at prayer, and if New Age baby boomers tend to be psychically-oriented meditators at workshop, then these "oral folk" practice a faith of trust and assurance at the traditional gatherings of communal churches.

The implications of this for ministry are enormous. In counseling, for example, the direction needs to be more like "folk healing," by which I mean small, communal groups of people who come together, not so much to examine inner feelings and thoughts, but to tell their stories to each other and to do that in a context where commitment to each other and a commitment to different ways of living enables them to cope and change. The strength of their faith, the support of the group, and their identity with these give them the power "to hunker down" and "make it through the night."

The implications for preaching are obvious—sermons oriented toward introspection and toward psychic analysis of some kind are alien. To be sure, sermons *do* need to be emotionally expressive, but not emotionally introspective. Yet, these are only suggestive implications. Such insights into oral culture have major import for Christian education, for devotional life, and—dear me—for spiritual formation. In fact, the latter has become much too bourgeois in the United States and involves far too much consciousness aerobics for people in traditional orality. Even the language, *spiritual formation*, will sound to them like the talk of a "dandy."

Operational and Situational versus Categorical Thinking

Aleksandr Luria was a fine Russian psychologist who did research on "illiterate" oral peasants in the Soviet Union. He wanted to know how these people did their thinking. In order to do so he devised a research tool which consisted of presenting his test subjects with four objects at a time. However, three of the objects belonged to one category and the fourth to another. The people in the experiment were asked to group similar objects or those which could be named by a single word. For example, in one group the peasants were presented with separate drawings of a hammer, saw, log, and hatchet. These oral people consistently thought of such items not in categorical terms—three tools with the log in another category—but rather in terms of practical situations. They did situational thinking of how these might be used in a very pragmatic way. "If you are a workman with tools and see a log, you think of applying the tool to it, not of keeping the tool away from what it was made for—in some weird intellectual game."[6]

Findings like these cause me great concern when I think about the academic study of theology and its capacity to relate to people of a traditional orality. I say this as one who deeply appreciates the work of the church in intellectually attempting to understand the faith. In the literate cultures of the world, it would be a failure of witness to turn away from such attempts. The academic study of faith is key to this witness. At the same time, it is a witness that has been an abject failure in communicating the faith to traditional/oral people.

It also has to be said because, as strange as it seems, an enormous defensiveness arises in literate discourse when issues of orality are raised. I recently heard a speaker address issues about traditional/oral people in a way that attempted to privilege indigenous ministry in such settings. Quite frankly, I was simply amazed at the inability of a number of "academically oriented" people in the audience to *hear* him. I was also surprised at the seemingly incessant number of "yes, but..." arguments that in almost every case seemed extraordinarily concerned with defending the academic study of faith. This, as far as I am concerned, needs no defense; certainly none of that kind. In fact, a number of people in the room could not get past *their* concern about an anti-intellectualism in the wider culture that made such presentations dangerous and easily misunderstood.

It was like thunder later in the meeting when a quiet, soft-spoken Native American woman testified that she had sat through dozens of meetings where literate-oriented discussions of the faith had taken place, only to find in the discussions of that day a foreboding defensiveness about an approach to religious life that had characterized so much of her own tradition.

Surely there are legitimate concerns about anti-intellectualism in the culture, and know-nothing positions can be found in this society and others, but that is decidedly not what is proposed here. In fact, I am profoundly indebted to the academic study of religion in my attempt to understand faith among traditionally oral people. I often wonder though, if much of the defensiveness about orality comes from people who grew up in traditional families, used education to get away from that past, and then be-come deeply threatened when this "shut-down" dimension of their lives resurfaces. But this is mainly conjecture on my part.

What is often missed in examining the beliefs of oral cul-tures is how radically concrete and operational these views are. There is no "distance" between what is going on and the activity of God and the forces of evil. These beliefs are immediately grounded and operative. Failure, struggle, death, separation, di-vorce, disability, loss of job, financial hardship and ruin, bleak tomorrows—all of these can be seen directly as God's plan—even as a trial and testing to call one toward a patient and rugged faithfulness in the valley of the shadow.

I have seen traditionally oral people face down grotesque human situations and take up challenges of heroic magnitude because God calls them to be victors in Christ. This confidence in God, *no matter what*, gets expressed by oral people in proverbs and stories, and in very concrete operational language: "One day at a time, sweet Jesus"; "To make a way outa no way"; "There's a way through even when there ain't a way out"; "No event is more powerful than God"; "God won't give you more than you can bear"; "This is a time of trial, and it serves a greater pur-pose"; "His eye is on the sparrow, and I know he watches me"; "There must be a heaven somewhere"; "Precious Lord, take my hand"; "God bats last"; "You just gotta trust God"; "God took my child so that she could be in heaven"; and the phrase of that wonderful folk theologian who told me, "God's coming, and He's gonna kick ass!"

I hasten to add that such faith is not typically narcotic. Some of it is, of course, but no more so than those pathetic es-capes into individualism, privatism, and subjectivity so charac-teristic of the privileged. It is not the special province of the religion of the disinherited to run from the world. They cannot afford to. Besides, religion is no longer the dominant opiate of the people in America; applied behavioral science is.

If one wants to counter the most indefensible proverbs and stories in such oral traditions, the way to do so is not to move in the direction of greater abstraction or to turn toward more com-pelling discourse, it is rather to articulate a more comprehensive proverb, a more powerful reality-constructing story.

This kind of operational and situational thinking is seen not only in faith claims, but also in morality. For traditional/oral people what is moral is often clear and unambiguous. Ethically speaking, there is not a lot of gray. Something is right or it is wrong. Morality is not thought of in abstract categories. Again, it deals with proverbs more than with principles, with stories more than with systematic explanations, and with practices more than with theoretical discussions of the good and the right.

At the operational and situational level, morality concerns things one says and does. It takes on quite concrete practices, such as, don't drink, smoke, curse, run with bad people, or carouse. To be sure, all of these are violated by traditional/oral people from time to time, but I am struck by the fact that even most of those who do drink too much, so often think they ought not. My recent research introduced me to hard-living people who have histories of drug abuse, troubled domestic relationships, and for some, jail records. Nevertheless, they tend to see morality in terms of very basic practices like those above and speak about someday getting things "straightened out" and "doing things right."

Such morality is much less dependent on the detailing of the complex factors that constitute competing claims in the vortex of a highly situated moral decision. One does not tend to struggle, therefore, with situational ethics most of the time. Morality is about *being* good, it is about practicing what is right. The result is that morality is not something one *thinks* about a great deal, it is something one *does* in regularized and understood conduct that is ongoing. To be sure, one thinks that such patterns are right and good, but one does not usually struggle with conflicting conceptions of the good in any abstract sense, nor with the right in forms of universal principles, except perhaps as these take proverbial form. Instead, you try to be a good neighbor, to help people out when they need it, to do what you say you will do, to be reliable, to be a good worker, to be a good American.

Please understand, I realize that there are traditional/oral people who don't give a damn about being moral. They are as capable of unethical lives as anyone. Rather, my point is that the morality traditional/oral people do live out tends to take this very concrete, operational, and life-situated form.

I used to work in the oil fields with Snooks Britt, a favorite "teacher" of mine. One day he asked me, with some contempt and confrontation aforethought, what "the college perfessors" were saying nowadays about sex outside marriage. Mind you, Snooks was not inordinately committed to moral conduct, but he enjoyed immensely "deconstructing" the views of college people he claimed "don't know anything about the real world. All they know is what they get out of books."

I was stuck because I really did not know what to say. I had read several books on sexual ethics that were helpful, but I did not know how to say something in the few words I knew Snooks would let me have before interrupting.

"Well, Snooks," I said, "you have to look at the human values at stake and the relationship of sex to the human good and the symphony of human values a person is to live out and fulfill."

"Aw, fuck that, college boy, is that the bullshit they are telling you at that little ole school up there? No wonder that you don't know whether to shit or go blind. Let me put it to you plain and simple. It's easy, it ain't hard. The answer is 'just don't fuck around'."

For the rest of that week we dug a ditch, hammering away with a pick at stone-hard, packed, oil-slicked Mississippi gravel so that we could "gather" those rock-like, earthen chips on a shovel we used like a dust pan. It was a hundred-yard ditch that took us five days to dig. But all that week I burned with frustration that Snooks's answer was so much closer to how we actually lived than my abstract answer. All that week I could not think of a way to introduce the power of his answer into ethical discourse at the college. They really were two different worlds. In a sense, I have spent my life trying to understand them and trying to be faithful to both.

I know Snooks's answer is not adequate to withstand the barrage of critical investigations it would be subjected to in an intellectual encounter. Yet, I have known utterly brilliant people who understood the major schools of ethical thought but whose emotional, professional, and marital lives were wrecked for the lack of a clear-cut practice. In spite of all their intellectual sophistication, they could have been "saved" by simply following the practice stated by Snooks in such earthy terms. At the same time,

I have seen the wisdom of oral morality itself become "abstract" and bring unspeakable harm when the conventions of behavior became more important than the people they were meant to serve.

It seems, then, that what is needed is work on an indigenous morality that is concrete, operational, and contextually situated; a morality that can be "critiqued" and can address the challenges that will inevitably come. We shall turn more explicitly to this question in the next chapter.

3

Loving Jesus and Justice: Doing Ethics with Traditional/Oral People

I was on a panel with a very prominent theologian, one whom I have always respected a great deal and still do. I had done a presentation on traditional/oral people, and he and I were responding to comments from the floor and directing questions to each other. At one point he turned to me and said:

"Tex, you can't just describe and defend these traditional ways. They have to be critical, too. These folks are being eaten alive in this culture. They cannot carry on without doing careful analysis and critique. They have to learn to do critical reflection. Otherwise, they are dead."

At the time I agreed with him because I respected him so much and because I, quite simply, had not thought about any alternative at that time. Yet, I remember a discomfort at that moment, sensing that I had not adequately responded. When I have an experience like that, I know that I need to give a subject further thought. As I began to delve more deeply into the research and the studies, a very different picture emerged.

On Being Non-Critical

I learned that traditional/oral people are non-critical in the sense that they do not make a theoretical critique. They do question a great many things. A friend of mine once said that he may not know a lot of fancy words or be real smart (actually he is), but he knew "the difference between a rain storm and somebody pissing on my boots!" I don't know a more graphic way to say that these traditional/oral people can tell when something is wrong and, when they do, can often comment on it in very colorful ways.

Still, when people think in proverbs, stories, and relationships, they do not "do" critique. To be sure, they do some other things, but they are not critiques, as such. Critique is closely tied to literate ways and to discourse, but it is not indigenous to oral, traditional people. While ministry with such folk needs to challenge massive movements afoot against their lives, critical thought is not an effective way to do this.

Before turning to an alternative, let me suggest some of the reasons why traditional/oral people do not do critical thinking. First, critique comes out of thought that works through theory, propositions, and discourse while oral thought, as we have seen, works through proverbs, stories, and relationships. The literate thinking of a critique uses formal logic, a highly differentiated language gauged to nuance meaning in very careful subtleties, and typically requires long training in an academic setting. To be able to perform this practice, if you will, takes "study" instead of the "apprenticeship" I describe in the second chapter as being employed by traditional/oral people.

Second, critical thought attempts to be as explicit as possible while oral thought understands things tacitly. I remember how hard a time I had when I first started writing in college. The professor kept telling me I had to say directly what I meant. I remember answering that any half-bright reader would know what I meant. But he would always reply that writing did not work that way: "You have to say exactly what you mean." However, in the oral culture in which I grew up, we understood most things tacitly. The local situation itself, with the rich offerings of its specific context, was sufficient.

The professor also taught that I must say what I did *not* mean. I remember the sense of provocation I felt. I thought that a reader would have to be completely out of it to think that I intended certain things just because I did not exclude them. I learned through hard experience that he was right.

Third, and probably even more important to consider is the workaday actuality of what oral people do and the fact that critique, as such, is not a part of that world. It is not a world where the emphasis is on the exactitude of language. With the concrete, practical focus of their world, the language they use is "plain talk," not "fancy talk." They are often suspicious of "big words" and "highfalutin ideas." Such words and ideas are what "the college boys" use and/or the boss uses (or the doctor or lawyers or the teachers down at the school or the new minister just out of seminary). The ideas may be vague but the control these words represent and their demeaning effect on traditional/oral people are quite real.

Still, a fourth factor runs even deeper than this. Given the highly concrete and practical character of their lives, there is a very basic suspicion of theory and, with it, a sense of critique as much ado about nothing. Traditional/oral people believe that life is deeper than theory. It simply does not line up with their lives.

Four years ago Peggy and I decided to do some home improvements. One of the projects was to move my study out of our bedroom, where it had been for nearly twenty years, and into the former bedroom of one of our adult, and now gone, children. The contractor, a man named Rick, came to the house one day to lay a vinyl floor that looked for the world like darkly stained oak.

"Would you like to see me lay this, Tex?" he asked, knowing I was a very amateur carpenter after he had straightened out a great many of my previous attempts over the three weeks he had worked there.

"You bet," I replied, grateful that I did not have to ask and would not worry that, if I had watched otherwise, he might think I was checking up on him.

Rick popped a chalk line down the middle of the room in each direction, making a large **X** and dividing the floor into four equal squares. Then he said:

"Now, Tex, if you ever do this yourself, remember to lay these strips of vinyl three-sixteenths of an inch off center."

"Whoa, Rick, why would you do that?"

"Well, it just works that way."

"That doesn't make sense. You have four equal squares in

the room at ninety degree angles and these vinyl strips are ninety degree angle rectangles. It won't match up if you lay the strips off center."

"I know it doesn't make sense."

"I don't understand that."

"I don't either, but if you want it to look right and to come out right, that's the way you have to do it. I don't understand it; I just know it works that way."

That day I watched Rick lay those vinyl strips three-sixteenths of an inch "off." The floor looks beautiful and straight as a die. In the concrete world with all the practical requirements that traditional/oral people face, life really is deeper than theory. One may argue, of course, that Rick is using theory, only a new theory, but it breaks with every thing he knows about math and measurement (not to mention his own common sense). Doubtless, too, there is a way to explain this anomaly in terms of theory, but such an interest is simply not yet, at least, relevant to Rick's work and life.

Fifth, theory, propositional thought and discourse are things that experts do, and traditional/oral people learned a long time ago to distrust experts. Experts are "outsiders." The problem here is not that traditional/oral people are "ingrown," though some are, of course, but that traditional people around the world have probably had as much experience with "other people" as anyone. They cannot move into insulated lifestyle enclaves; they are too much "in the way" of modernity and progress, and modernity and progress always bring their experts with them.

The major problems with experts are that they seem inevitably to bring someone else's agenda with them and that they want to do something *to* traditional local people, no matter how much they protest to the contrary. They always have "a better idea," and they tend to represent power, the kind that represents control over local folk.

Experts also have a comical side because they never seem to agree. Nothing delights traditional people more than stories about experts who cannot get together about what is going on and what needs to be done. Folklore is full of narratives about experts, their fancy foibles, their mammoth mistakes, their unfailing unfitness, and their obvious obfuscation of ordinary life.

Ed Kail teaches town and country ministry at Saint Paul and tells the story of a baboon whose cage fell off the circus train. The poor creature was killed instantly. Later, a couple of farmers came by and attempted to determine what kind of critter it was. One of them finally concluded that, from the looks and the location of its calluses, it must have been a seminary professor.

Finally, to traditional people there are as many opinions as experts, and they suspect that the reason for such diversity grows from the variety of interests they represent. They know, too, that many experts can't make up their own minds. Harry Truman captured this perfectly when he said that he wanted a one-armed economist in the White House. When asked why, he answered that he was tired of hearing economists say: "Well, on the one hand . . . , but on the *other* hand."

It is, therefore, easy to understand why traditional/oral people do not use discourse and why they so often distrust people who do. More than that, it is clear why it is hard to do social ethics and to engage systemic social issues in a discursive way. The job now is to discover an alternative approach to social ethics that is indigenous and compelling.

Toward a Traditional/Oral Social Ethic

Early one morning I was standing in my office when Julie came by. She was one of the best custodians we ever had. A kind and genial woman in her forties, she worked hard to do her job well. She would drop by my office every now and then to exchange pleasantries.

"Tex, you got a minute?"

"Sure, come on in."

"Do you mind if I close the door?"

"No, not at all. Sit down."

"I'd rather stand," she said in a kind of halting way. She started a sentence about three different ways but could not complete it. Then she said, "Do you mind if I ask you a personal question, I mean, is it all right?"

After I gave her several assurances that it would be fine, she almost blurted it out: "Are those your grandchildren in the picture over there, the ones in the kimonos?"

"Yes, they are our son Shawn's children." Our son had the good sense to marry Enami Nagakura, a woman from Japan whom he met at Arizona State, and their two children and our daughter Jennifer's two make up four of "the most adorable grandchildren in the world." At Christmastime the year before, Ena sewed two colorful kimonos, took the children's picture in them, and gave us one of the pictures for a present.

"Are they Oriental?" asked Julie, now seeming to gain a bit of confidence about what she wanted to say.

"Yes, they are Japanese-American." I responded. "The oldest is named Mellisa Nagakura Sample and the youngest is named Jessica Mai. Ain't that a kick?"

"Well, do you . . . I mean . . . you must feel okay about different races marrying?"

"Well, sure. It can be tough on the couple, but when two people genuinely love each other it can be beautiful."

"Hmm, let me ask another question. How do you feel about black people?"

"This is certainly no time for white folks to be bragging about their liking for black people, not with all that's gone on, but I like to think that I care about black folks."

"Whew!" Julie said in sudden relief. "I thought you would, but I wasn't sure, but when I saw that picture of those children I figured I could ask you about it. I just thought you would know what it felt like. Could I show you some pictures of my grandchildren?"

Julie's son had married an African-American woman and they had two of "the most beautiful grandchildren in the world." Julie had not been at the seminary very long, and was dying to show the pictures, but was not sure how they would be received. But notice what she said after making sure that the two children in the picture were my grandchildren: *"I just thought you would know what it felt like."*

This story illustrates what the rest of this chapter is about. An important question with people who think in proverbs, stories, and relationships is how they do ethics, especially social ethics. It is an important question because my theological colleague calling for critical thought is exactly right about how traditional/oral people are being eaten alive. While I do not share his confidence in critical thought for such folks because it is not indigenous, it is nevertheless crucial that a native way to do social ethics be found; an approach not like that in the academy, but one nevertheless able to deal with issues of social justice and social goods.

The Empathic Core

The story about my friend, Julie, can help us to see an indigenous way to do ethics. Note what she said: "I just thought you would know what it felt like." The presence of the pictures, the intuition she had that a grandfather of interracial children could empathize with her situation, led her to raise the question. This matter of empathy is crucial to understanding morality— probably for any one—but especially for traditional/oral people who do not think in propositions, theory, and discourse.

Martin Hoffman maintains that this empathic capacity comes early in moral development, beginning as an emotional response to simple perceptual experience. He defines empathy as "an affect (feeling) response more appropriate to someone else's situation than to one's own."[1] The story has been around for years about the child who told her mother that she had found another little girl sitting on the curb crying. When her mother asked her what she did, the little girl responded: "I just sat down and cried with her." Hoffman himself reports the incident of a seventeen-month-old boy who watched a physician give another child a shot and reacted angrily by hitting the doctor.[2]

It would be a mistake, however, to equate empathy only with early development. Hoffman discusses mature empathy, an advanced level that is subtle, complex, and capable of sensitive, affective distinctions that can contribute to informed moral judgments. My point is that the morality of traditional/oral people can be quite mature. So I am not discussing some second-rate form of morality. The emphases of moral development theorists like Kohlberg have focused too much on cognitive and reasoning processes and have ignored feelings. Such work not only privileges certain male tendencies; it is also captive to class and to literate expression. For him to call his stages of moral development "universal" is simply ludicrous.

This empathic core is found in a host of sayings not far from any conversation of traditional/oral people. They use phrases like "I just felt sorry for them"; "I know how it would make me feel"; "You could see just how badly it hurt her"; and so on. I have always been struck by how important the Golden Rule is for them: "Do to others as you would have them do to you." It is a teaching that captures the place of empathy in moral life.

I have known clergy and academics who have been critical of this teaching, arguing that it lacks precision and that it does not deal adequately with people who want the wrong things for themselves. Such critique, however, does not pay sufficient attention to the tacit understanding of traditional/oral people, on the one hand, and is not adequately attentive to the central role of empathy and how much the Golden Rule speaks to their moral sense, on the other. Further, the mature expression of it found in traditional/oral people is a resource for ethics, not a detriment.

Communal Knowing

Hoffman points out that in early development this empathy takes on a cognitive dimension. The child learns to identify with the feelings of others by living through similar situations with them. Thus, empathy and knowing develop together. That is, as the child goes through early experiences with parents and other members of the family, she learns from this interaction what her mother feels if she drops something on her toe. If a child grows up in a truly communal setting, he also experiences a host of opportunities to learn empathetically what others feel. The point is that the knowing develops through these communal relationships.

Thinking in Relationships

I am also interested in how important these early experiences and history are for people who mature, but who continue to think in relationships. When a question is asked, when an issue is posed, relational thinking begins to function in terms of how the question or issue will affect those in the communal web of relationships. We are looking here at a whole way of framing life and its forms. It is a way to engage the world, to live communally, and to give life meaning and value. Something like this, obviously more thickly complex and immensely diverse than I am able to convey here, is the way most traditional and oral people have grown to maturity and lived out their lives.

Storytelling

Moreover, this empathy and these communal relationships are deepened and extended through the telling of the stories of the family. Our grandchildren are staying with us this week. Almost every day they ask me to retell a story from the family that they have heard their father, or someone else, recount. These are not children in a communal setting, but all week I have been impressed with how important the storytelling is and how central it is to building their worlds. It is difficult to exaggerate its importance for more traditional/oral people.

Proverbs

In oral and traditional cultures the empathy, the stories, and the relationships, clothed in tacit understanding, crystallize in proverbs. These proverbs are not simply clichés in these settings, but are "short sayings learned through hard experience." They become keys for bunching up experience, for reminding people of what needs to be done or, perhaps more important, for providing reasons for why something is done.

This picture of traditional morality is admittedly too simple, but the highly complex dimensions of traditional/oral morality can be seen as the interaction of these five central ingredients: empathy, communal knowing, relational thinking, stories, and proverbs.

Let's go back to Julie for a minute. We have seen how important empathy was for her. Note, too, how key it was that she suspected that the girls were family (a kind of communal knowing) and how her relational thought moved to a conclusion on the matter of interracial marriage. Later in our conversation she also gave it proverbial closure when she said in leaving: "When it's family, it's okay." She did not mean "in the family, anything goes." If she had meant this, she would have said it. She's plenty bright. She knows the difference. In her tacit understanding she has a place for all kinds of exceptions and for moral direction. No discursive critique of her saying is appropriate or necessary.

Moreover, in saying, "When it's family, it's okay," she is not denying interracial marriage for people *not* family. Rather, she is giving interracial marriage legitimation of the first order.

Doing Ethics in a Traditional/Oral Way

What I want to do now is to take these dimensions of traditional morality and demonstrate how each is used in doing ethics on a traditional, oral, and indigenous model. First, such an ethic must touch this empathic core. This can be done in myriad ways. Sometimes it is done through a story. I like to call this "the perceptive story." Such stories personalize people and situations, and put the listeners in the settings so that their own stories participate in the event and pose the questions and issues in ways directly related to their own lives.

Second, and closely related to the above, is the job of connecting an ethical issue to basic communal relationships. Stories can do this, but so can proverbs. Proverbs often elicit basic relationships in one's life because the teaching is so tied to a certain person. Equally compelling is the skill of being able to offer the right proverbial word at the right time. Sister Ann Nielsen tells a wonderful story she heard in Africa where she has been a missionary and has collected several thousand proverbs. A man from Malawi left his tribal home to go and make money. He was away for three years and made no contact with his wife. Upon his return, his wife had a child that was clearly not his. Wanting to divorce his wife and take all her belongings, the husband took her to court. She was defended by an uncle, who won the case with what seems to have been a proverbial coup. He said: "If you leave your hoe in the rain for three years, it will rust." Sister Nielsen explains that the court realized that the wrong done was not the wife's unfaithfulness, but the husband's abandonment and lack of support. To the degree that one can touch these communal relations with proverbs, stories, a relational thought, or something else about the integrity or the violation of these ties, one has moved into a powerful moral "logic" that is all the more compelling because of its indigenous character.

Third, the capacity to tell stories and to make moral argument in narrative form is a profound ethical skill. Hardly anything has such moral legitimation and persuasion. John Milbank argues that story is more basic than theory and discourse.[3] While one may challenge this claim—I do not—it would be difficult to argue against it with traditional/oral people who think in stories. What this usually means is that oral people go through a story in their minds to sort out the moral questions. Some call this scenario thinking. That is, one story triggers a story in the listener, and the listener thinks through her own story, the communal relations it entails, and the empathic associations connected with it. It genuinely is a system for thinking about ethics; one with enormous power.[4]

Finally, as I have said, proverbs crystallize these learnings and they become a part of the oral tradition and available to the community. These proverbs in an oral community have enormous complexity, and, of course, not everyone can use them with equal skill. Over time, the community will look to certain people to provide this service. Such people take on the role of moral sages or holy people. I have known such people in churches, neighborhoods, and communities all my life. I grew up in a taxicab stand, and I remember very well the people who were sages. We waited for them to give the word at a crucial point in a conversation, an argument, or after an event. It is an old practice and continues in the midst of this society today.

These then are the basic dimensions of traditional morality. Perhaps a story can "summarize" them. In the sixties a friend of mine was involved in the civil rights movement, and it put no little strain on his relation with his mother and father. Once he and his dad were in the meanest disagreement they had ever had. While they often argued about civil rights, their basic relationship never seemed up for grabs. On this day, however, they had both gotten very heated, and my friend Teddy worried to himself he was about to lose his relationship to his father. He reports:

"I was also not being persuasive. What happened next was not something I thought my way to, and to this day I don't know how it came to me except that I think it came from God. At the moment when our argument became most fierce, I blurted out to my dad: 'Daddy, when you get to heaven, what are you going to tell Teddy Mae Rogers about all the terrible things you have said about her children?'"

You need to understand that Teddy Mae Rogers was born a slave in the early 1860s. When my friend Teddy's father was born in 1905, his mother's milk was no good and Teddy Mae Rogers suckled him.

She partly raised him, and even in that context Teddy maintains that his father loved her very much. His father decided to name his first child "Teddy Mae." When his son came along with the wrong "plumbing," he named him "Teddy," not Theodore.

After Teddy blurted out his question, his dad said angrily: "What the hell are you talking about now? Have you completely lost your mind? You see, this civil rights stuff is affecting your brain."

"No, Daddy, I'm serious," Teddy argued back, "You are talking about Teddy Mae Rogers's children. I mean, her children and grandchildren and great-grandchildren are all over the United States. They're in Houston and Beaumont and St. Louis and Cleveland and Chicago and New York and Philadelphia. They are all over this country. They are the people you are talking about. When you get to heaven and see her, what are you going to tell her about the mean things you say about her children?"

It stopped him cold.

"I had never before stopped my dad in my life, and I really don't take credit for this one," he reports. "I don't know where it came from, but Dad just stood there for a long time. I think I know exactly what was going on in his head. Suddenly, he was in heaven, face to face with Teddy Mae Rogers, and she was asking him the question."

This is what some people mean by scenario thinking. Teddy's dad was trying to sort out what he would say to her and, apparently, was not coming up with very many answers. After what seemed like an interminable silence, his father simply murmured "Hmm" and left the room.

"Now that was almost thirty years ago," Teddy continues, "and Dad and I have had many arguments since, and I have never again stopped him. But we have never had *that* argument, not even one other time."

Teddy's question touched his father at the point of his

deepest empathies, named as basic a relationship as he had that went back to his earliest communal and family ties, engaged him in a serious imaginative narrative with Teddy Mae Rogers in heaven, and, I suspect, brought on a raft of proverbs having to do with gratitude, speaking well of the dead, repaying life and death debts, faithfulness to "family," the relationship of this life to the next, the capacity of one's sins to find one out, and the watchful eye of God on the events of this world.

Traditional/Oral Morality and Social Justice

The charge typically made against traditional/oral people is that they are too parochial, too focused on their "own people," and therefore not open to wider issues of social justice. I believe this is a human problem, not one specific to oral and traditional people only, although it may pose the issue in different ways for different groups.

The more important question is whether traditional/oral people can do social ethics that attend to justice issues beyond their local, communal relationships. I think so, and, in this last section, we'll find that the job is to see how. Again, empathy, communal knowing, relational thinking, stories, and proverbs form the framework in which such an approach to ethics will occur. How can such a framework be used to expand the range of concerns so that more systemic issues can be addressed? Or, to say it differently, can one use indigenous local practices of morality to examine systemic issues?

I not only say yes, I want to argue that this framework is a resource that far too much work in social ethics has ignored, the result being that an important impact of the discipline has been lost at precisely the point where it has been needed most. Too much ethics is written for the academy and not nearly enough for the workaday lives of people.

In terms of ministry, when clergy can only do social ethics in the frameworks of theory and discourse, entire arenas of ministry are squandered. This society is in too much trouble for clergy to forego such a massive opportunity to engage people in the profound social and moral questions of the times.

To demonstrate this use of an oral approach to social ethics,

I want to examine some of the impact of global capitalism on the relocation of industries, the loss of jobs, and the potentiality for such events to become the occasion for self-blame and/or racist scapegoating.

Let's say that Joe is an auto worker in Kansas City who makes $30,000 a year and Mary, his spouse, works as a clerk and earns $8,000. They do okay. Then the news comes that the assembly plant where Joe works is moving to the Maquiladora area of Mexico. Joe loses his job but finally finds another one making only $15,000 a year. A narrative begins to develop about the hardships they have in terms of holding on to their house, their beginning to borrow money that will be difficult to repay, the conflicts in their marriage brought on by financial strain, and Joe's own questioning of himself—although he is obviously not responsible for his situation. The future looks bleak.

Such a narrative as this, one that speaks directly to the circumstances of working people's lives and those of others, engages oral people at a bone-deep level. This situation can be an occasion for an attack on the working people of Mexico, deflecting anger on them that doubtlessly could be better aimed elsewhere. How can one get a more human view of Mexican working people in such a situation with people who are communal and local?

The best way is to tell a realistic story about Maria and José in Mexico that depicts their workaday world in ways that can touch the empathic core of working people here. For example, Maria works in the job that Joe once had, but she makes only a few dollars a day. José works as a carpenter and stonemason, but both of them together cannot make ends meet. They have children and child care problems, as do Joe and Mary.

Stories like these connect with the empathic core of oral people. By working from the communal relationship of Joe and Mary, one can then expand this story beyond Joe and Mary to others like Maria and José. The crusher in this scenario is that neither family can afford to buy a new car like the ones Joe used to make and Maria makes now. The proverbial clincher comes in the country music song: "A working man [woman] can't get nowhere today."

A thickly descriptive, perceptive story does several things.

First, it is an indigenous practice in itself. Second, it expands the range of the empathic core. Third, in moving from one set of communal relations to another it engages in the very relational thinking that is so key—along with thinking in stories—in oral practice. And, finally, when a proverb "summarizes" the matter, especially in lyrics from music loved by the local people, one has a strong moral base from which to work with the issue.

I realize we have not yet engaged the ethical issue fully. So far, we have only placed the systemic question in an implicative narrative form. This, however, opens the door to a fuller examination. While I have some disagreement with the United States Roman Catholic Bishops' Pastoral Message and Letter, "Economic Justice for All: Catholic Social Teaching and the U.S. Economy," it received a lot of attention nationally. Because of this and because of its general accessibility, I want to use it briefly in terms of the story about the move of the assembly plant.

The section of the Pastoral message on "Employment" is virtually a catalogue of the issues involving Joe, Mary, Maria, and José. It poses basic questions that easily take on narrative form in their situation. Take, for example, the subsection in the Pastoral message on "Unemployment in a Changing Economy." It addresses the issues of the changing structure of the economy of the United States in terms of such matters as technological change, the downgrading and displacement of workers, the increase of service-sector jobs with low pay and little or no benefits, increased competition in world markets, and the movement of capital, technology, and jobs to foreign sites. My point is that these systemic ethical issues can be addressed in very concrete and narrative forms that utilize communal relationships to get at systemic issues: personal stories for people to think through and that touch their hearts (the empathic core), and telling proverbs to nail down the point.

Moreover, it is not my intention to leave the impression that these changes in the U.S. economy are simply the outgrowth of massive, impersonal forces moving above human will and agency. In some cases these moves are motivated by unconscionable greed in an idolatrous lust for profit that cannot be squared with any defensible view of the common good, either in the United States or in the countries to which the corporation moves its factories. Here, the narratives of what happened (who made the decision, the cooperation of government officials, decisions by the board of directors and the CEO, and so on) become not only highly useful data for moral condemnation, but can constitute social analysis needed for change.

At the same time, while I find much of what corporate America is doing in the Maquiladora area to be indefensible, one must also, in fairness, take into account the pressured decisions many corporate leaders now face in an increasingly complex world market. Some of their decisions result from systemically determined choices narrowed by the market contexts in which they work and live. Here again, perceptive stories of executives as real people making hard decisions can not only bring even greater realism to issues but can also speak powerfully to the systemic character of the problem and the necessity of systemic responses to economic questions that cannot be reduced to human egoism and profit-mongering alone.

This too-brief development of the use of a traditional oral approach to examine a systemic ethical issue, nevertheless, indicates what can be done. Such an approach to ethics is not a detriment but becomes an even more concrete and effective way to address these concerns than an approach that remains abstract and unconnected to the specific lives of people so radically affected by contemporary events.

An indigenous social ethic, of course, raises the question of social change. Here, too, the issue of native practices becomes of paramount significance. We turn to these matters next.

4

We Never Did It That Way Before: Tradition, Resistance, Subversion, and Change

Thirty-five and a solid student, Tom had the gifts and graces for ministry. He possessed a pastor's heart and exuded that special quality that communicated his outright commitment to people. All the more reason, then, that I should have been so surprised when he told me what he wanted to do for his class project that term. A senior, he had served for two years at a church with an average attendance of forty-five, up twenty-five percent since he had started there. It was a family-size church, made up of very traditional/oral people.

"Tex, I want to do my class project on management by objectives."

"Tom, you can't do that. M.B.O. simply isn't appropriate for a congregation the size and character of yours."

"Wait a minute, my people voted 100 percent in the board meeting last night to do this. They want to do it. Are you telling me they can't?"

"No, of course not, but it's not an appropriate procedure for a church like yours."

"Look, Tex, they want to do it, and I want to. Why not?" Reluctantly, I agreed to the project. In typical fashion he did it well. We kept in touch throughout the project, and I could see that he had the utmost cooperation of the church. His well-done paper reported the process with a final section on the future: a timeline, a budget, and assignments of committees and officers to get the various jobs done. I was pleased with how much he read, the thoroughness of the process, and the report itself.

About two years later I ran into a couple of people from the church. As we exchanged pleasantries, I asked about the congregation and how things were going. They reported that it was fine and soon began to talk about Tom.

"We sure miss Tom. He was such a fine pastor. Don't misunderstand, we love our new pastor, and we will love him more as time goes on. But Tom was just special. We will always remember him."

I agreed about Tom's special talents and could not resist asking about how the M.B.O. program was going.

"Oh, that . . . , well, we kind of dropped it after Tom left. He was so interested in that stuff and wanted to do it so badly that a group of us got together before a board meeting and agreed that if Tom wanted to do it, we'd do it. One person said, 'Look, our pastor wants to get a degree and wants to learn how to do this management by objectives. We love him and if he wants to do it, by golly, we're gonna do it. Heck, we can hold our noses and breathe under water if we have to.'"

If one has to choose, I would rather have someone like Tom, even doing M.B.O. in a church like that, than someone who did not have his relational skill and compassion. At the same time, Tom's inexperience and misplaced enthusiasm set in sharp relief a range of practices in terms of organizational and social change that are externally imposed on traditional and oral people. Models of change in this society come too often out of academic and corporate America. Too often these are not indigenous to the people where the changes are used, especially with traditional/oral people. They need the approaches to change that will come from the practices of traditional/oral people themselves.

Tradition and Social Change

No bias is more detrimental to the search for indigenous approaches to social change than the belief that traditional/oral people do not change. To be in virtually any session of professionals conferencing about traditional/oral people is to hear complaints about how resistant they are to anything new. They are "stuck in their ways," "hold on to the past," "are resistant to new ideas," creatures of "unreflective habits." What is so often absent from such professional myopia is any sense that the professional's own values are not "universal," but in fact are in service to modernity and represent a commitment to changes of a certain kind that reflect an agenda external to the traditional/oral community and serving neither its interests nor its values.

What is quite clear is that traditional/oral people do change. They always have. If humans have been on the earth for about a million years, and if written history is only about four to five thousand years old, then the overwhelming mass of human existence was lived in traditional/oral communities. Over the course of all that time a great deal of change has occurred. Only a generalized gloss of human experience, not a thickly descriptive account of the primal societies still around, could miss the enormous range of challenges to a tradition and its response to them.

For example, Terence Ranger reports that the Mwari priests and the spirit mediums in Zimbabwe often condemned innovations in African agriculture, but it turned out that they were condemning entrepreneurial obligations that separated the achiever from his collective obligations.[1] Ranger makes it clear that rural religion in early colonial Zimbabwe was not simply some ongoing outdated beliefs and practices, but was rather a struggle between both European and African traditions. In this case, rural religion directly addressed the "new business" of being a peasant.

The real question is not *whether* traditional/oral people change. The question is *how*. The beginning of an answer lies in the way tradition typically is used. This use counters the notion that traditional people are slavish in their devotion to tradition. Walter Ong makes the point that *the integrity of the past serves the integrity of the present.*[2] All people constantly face new problems, new crises, and new issues. The scenario of traditional/oral people living in some idyllic state of suspended stability not only misrepresents the experience of many people in the United States, it grossly misconstrues the circumstances of people in more primal societies. Ong does not mean to suggest, and I do not, that traditional/oral people are utterly rational and utilitarian in their orientation to tradition. Perhaps the key word here is

integrity. By "integrity" he means the force that keeps together
the unity and wholeness of the web of relations that constitute
the community. The "integrity of the present" conveys the importance of the community and the extended relations that constitute it *now*. The past is used to sustain this integrated
wholeness in terms of the challenges it faces in the present. This
is an integrity rooted in tradition and is in deep continuity with
it, but it is also a tradition*ing*, and this story, if I may move to a
metaphor, continues to take form and change as the story goes
on. In the twists and turns of the narrative, tradition is used to
face the challenges and changes that inevitably appear in the
present. So it is not a matter of simply doing what was done in
the past, but of using the past to deal with the present in order to
sustain communal life.

Let me be clear, too, that this does not mean that tradi-
tional/oral people are always making the best and most humane
use of tradition. They can, of course, hold on to a practice too
long. They can fail miserably at facing the challenges before
them. Tradition does not relieve a people from the finitude and
foibles that characterize human societies everywhere.

Second, in the service of the tradition to the integrity of the
present, it is obvious that tradition is a very rich resource in most
human societies, and certainly so in our own. Any attempt at indigenous social change will recognize this resource and work
from it. It is not all of one piece, but is as rich in contradiction as
it is in continuity. Determining the mix of contradiction and continuity, of course, is an empirical process and varies from group
to group and from time to time.

Major voices and minor ones speak in its story. It has the
loud voices of an established consensus and the silent ones of
those marginal to its power. Nevertheless, for every story that
sustains a practice, there will be another one to challenge it and
call for a different response. For every proverb that leads to one
decision, another will call it into question and suggest a different
way. Finally, the claims of one set of relationships will, with any
matter of significant import, raise up claims of another kind from
yet other ties within the same community. Tradition is a resource
replete with a vast array of the things needed for indigenous
change. What will not work is external "human engineering"

coming in the Trojan horse of "progress" pretending to be a gift while bearing the destructive forces of a utilitarian mentality insensitive to and, usually, uncaring of the hospitality so commonly offered.

Third, we usually think of traditional/oral people as isolated. I suspect this reflects our own cultural ethnocentrism, rather than any accurate assessment. Such claims typically mean that these groups are not in relation to us! To whatever extent traditional peoples were in isolation before, and certainly some were, it is not true of the mass of people in the United States, and for that matter, most of the world. It is doubtful whether any traditional/oral people are completely isolated and independent anywhere in the world today. They often stand in the way of the ambitions of global capitalism's unquenchable thirst for new markets. Are such people more isolated than highly educated professionals and managers who work in offices and return to the residential enclaves of affluence? I doubt it.

Fourth, Anthony Giddens makes the point that it is more important to examine the contradictions a practice embodies than the functions it performs.[3] If one places too much stress on the functions of tradition, one misses the contradictions and their potential role in social change. We can look at only one example here, and perhaps the best one is the contradiction between tradition and modernity itself. Much of what goes on among traditional people is the struggle between the continuity of the past and the new challenges posed by contemporary events. Terence Ranger, in his study of rural Zimbabwe, points out the centrality of community in peasant consciousness and the importance of the village entity, but he also notes that the latter is a product of new forces. It changes with time; it is a social, historically constructed entity.

More than that, he includes David Sabean's observation that "what is common in community is not shared values or common understanding so much as the fact that members of a community are engaged in the same argument . . . in which alternative strategies, misunderstandings, conflicting goals and values are thrashed out."[4] These arguments and disagreements are, in part, the result of the struggle of the community with the invasive influences of modernity. A more accurate picture of what goes on here is the process of historical traditioning struggling with rapid social changes. It is a dynamic process filled with the contradictions of life lived on the ragged edges of things out of joint. It is a world of change, not of stability. Its continuity is in the ongoing story not in some reified ongoing consensus of values or some frozen traditional rigidity.

We Always Did It That Way Before: Authority, Resistance, and Subversion

Perhaps no single comment sends professionals into apoplexy quicker than the phrase, "We never did it that way before." This phrase is pervasive and long-lived, and is, in part, responsible for the negative views of traditional/oral people one finds among career-minded professionals.

The retort represents at least two things. The first of these is a direct claim that the people in question are committed to traditional authority. In searching for the legitimation of a decision or direction they look to tradition for a rationale. If these are older people in the church, they may very well think back to the Great Depression before considering a building project or some other large expenditure. The pastor may be very frustrated by this response that could very well impede ministry to new groups moving into the community, and thereby be detrimental to the mission of the church. In fairness, the proposal may also be one that serves the pastor—making him or her look good in a denominational dossier. Congregations know that pastors leave after a short time, and know that it is they who will be left with the responsibility. They bring, in this case, their memory of the Great Depression to this question and it provides its own kind of wisdom.

I do not mean to suggest that traditional/oral people are always correct. I remember a church of such folks in an inner city congregation whose sanctuary burned down leaving them with several hundred thousand dollars of insurance money. In trying to think about what direction the church needed to go and how the church might use the money in its mission, one board member seemed to speak for the congregation when he said he wanted to rebuild the sanctuary just the way it was. When asked why, and what he saw as the ministry of the church, he said: "I just want this church to stay alive long enough to bury me and my family from it." When asked where he found this understanding of the church in the New Testament, he said he did not care what the New Testament said.

It is not my intent to defend such behavior. Rather, I want to suggest that the way to approach issues of ministry in traditional congregations is from an authoritative tradition that reflects their story and the place it has in their lives. This is not, nor is anything else in this book, a panacea. My attempt is not to come up with ideas and practices that always work, but to suggest directions for an indigenous ministry.

The second thing that needs to be said about these appeals to "the way we always did things" is an understanding of their use as forms of resistance and subversion. Traditional/oral people know that these kinds of claims enormously frustrate pastors and other professionals. It is, therefore, important to see these claims as tactics and to appreciate the masterful forms of resistance they represent.

As stated earlier, traditional/oral people do not have positive histories with experts, professionals, and other representatives of "modern progress and development." They are more often exploited by such representatives and organizations who attempt to impose on them an agenda alien to their lives and their well-being. Even in the negative case presented above, the denominational representatives knew that these people would not live long and were looking ahead to the ministry of that church after the present congregation was dead and gone. "They," the church members, were not the primary concern. While the board member's argument was not a New Testament one and, as stated, indefensible in terms of faithfulness, I think if he had been presented with options that dealt with his own loyalties to that church and the future of the people in that congregation, his response might have been different. Perhaps not, but he would not have carried the day as he did.

We often fail to see that traditional/oral people are relatively powerless in the contemporary world. For many of them their story is one of grudging retreat before change that serves an efficient, utilitarian, and managed deployment of resources that serves profit. Resistance to the organizational criteria of career-minded professionals is basic to the lives of many people. The development of the new at the expense of the old is a very old story. Look at a few current examples: the loss of community schools in rural America; the dying of small businesses before the onslaught of Walmart, MacDonald's, and mega-malls; the loss of local autonomy to a nation-state whose tentacles of control reach into every community prescribing and proscribing local patterns in forms insensitive to their lifestyles; the changing of churches from gatherings of extended family to the coordinated programming of a differentiated small-group life; the shift of pastors from the role of parson to that of the administrative director of a religious business; and changes made in the texts of liturgy, song, and belief that contain some familiar words but seem strangely disconnected from the lives of the faithful. These are experiences all too well known to traditional/oral people. All of them happen in the midst of major shifts in cultural attitudes toward marriage, family, and sexuality. It would be strange, indeed, if traditional/oral people were not in considerable resistance to these local, national, and global events. Changes that threaten traditional life have gone on for centuries.

Therefore, it is not surprising that people use tradition as a weapon. In the face of modernity such uses are "weapons of the weak," to use James Scott's helpful phrase. Scott lists ordinary everyday weapons of resistance for powerless groups including such things as foot dragging, dissimulation, desertion, sabotage, false- or non-compliance, pilfering, feigned ignorance, slander, and arson. He observes that such actions require little coordination or planning, make use of informal networks and implicit understandings, value individual self-help, and avoid direct, symbolic confrontation with authority. Such resistance is usually very effective over the long run as it slowly nibbles policies to death.[5] Scott is demonstrating how these low-profile techniques are suited to the cultures he studies, but an experienced pastor can cite any number of instances of these tactics being used in every congregation of traditional/oral people ever served. Certainly one of the best uses of the weapons of the weak is to say "we never did it that way before."

Traditional Approaches to Social Change

The first step in doing indigenous change with traditional people is to recognize when resistance and protest occur. One of the key forms this takes is in these "weapons of the weak."

Resistance is a sign that something is wrong. One of the best ways to deal with such resistance is to re-examine one's approach to make sure it is indigenous. This section suggests forms this approach can take with traditional/oral people. When the strategy is indigenous, traditional/oral people will feel that the pastor or other leader is at least in touch with the community.

One clarification is in order here. I am not asking professionals to use traditional/oral models of change in order to become better at manipulating these people. My hope instead is that a deeper understanding of the place of tradition will lead to a greater appreciation of the people and of the wisdom carried in their stories.

It is not my pretension, however, that I come out of some neutral-value orientation that takes no stand on issues before the church and the society. For example, traditions, like more modern social constructions, carry destructive beliefs and practices and these must be challenged. From a Christian perspective destructive beliefs and practices like racism, sexism, and classism cannot be benignly ignored as though somehow tradition makes them harmless. We are to be "all things to all people," but as Paul said, "for the sake of the gospel" (1 Cor. 9:22–23). Beyond that we are not to be conformed to this world, but to be transformed (Rom. 12:2).

Indigenous change does not mean unfaithful accommodation to the status quo. The task of following Christ is for the Word to become flesh in the church, embodied in its corporate life. In addressing indigenous ministry here I am not discussing a diminution of the Word. Rather, I am asking what it means in John 1:14 that "the Word became flesh and dwelt" (RSV) or "lived among us" (NRSV). The Greek word literally translated means "to pitch tent." What does it mean to pitch tent with traditional/oral people and be faithful to the Word? Our call is to be faithful to that Word. Our mission as Christians is to bring commitments to the

Word in our ministry with anyone. So it is altogether appropriate to work for change with value commitments. Only the naive believe they are neutral. The question is whether these changes serve traditional people and the gospel or whether they serve some agenda of modernity and "progress" or the criteria for professional advancement for the clergy or other professional.

The Holistic Character of Communal Relations

When Claude Levi-Strauss writes that the savage mind totalizes, he refers to people in a primal society.[6] To be sure, these folk are quite different from the kind of traditional/oral people we find in the United States, but his point has genuine usefulness in understanding cultures in our own society. As we have seen, traditional people think in relationships, especially communal ones. Levi-Strauss's comment speaks to this.

David Hesselgrave reports on a study of children who were shown pictures of houses. They were merely line pictures of a three-sided box open at the top with an upside-down v for a roof: The houses had no windows or doors, no shrubs or plants, or sidewalks. In fact, the picture was composed of only five lines. They asked the children what was missing from the house. One little girl's immediate response was: "Where are the neighbors?"[7] This kind of relational and communal thinking is characteristic of traditional and oral people. This is one reason why they can be so frustrating to professionals. To the extent that such professionals think in linear terms about how to get things done, they will have difficulty understanding the complex multidimensional and lateral thinking of traditional people. In assessing a community situation they will find it necessary to think about the extended communal web of relationships. What happens to relatives and friends when a certain action is taken? How will this affect the feeling tone of the communal web of relations?

My point is not that professional and literate people are without concern about family and friends, but that they are usually more mobile geographically, less local in orientation, and not usually involved in extended communal relations. They tend to be more individualistic and their professional tasks are more goal-oriented than they are communally located and committed.

This means that their work will take on a more utilitarian character, be more linear in focus, and be less "complicated" by "lateral" and multidimensional communal concerns. For example, in a communal church of traditional/oral people a decision to begin raising the church budget through an every member canvass will not be considered on the basis of whether it will raise the most money, but on the effect it will have on people who have carried certain fundraising responsibilities in the past and whether they will perceive this decision to have shunted them aside. Professionals may concentrate on the effectiveness of the new program and the most rational use of the resources of the church. In fact, such churches will typically rotate jobs in a church so that the work can be more task-oriented and less relational in focus.

Add-On Change

Because of this heightened sensitivity to communal relationships, indigenous change in these settings does not proceed by dismantling this more holistic pattern. For one thing, it takes a long time to learn these relations and the implicit understandings and tacit knowledge that accompany them. Moreover, concern is more person-centered than analytical. In fact, analysis can be dangerous in oral and traditional settings. Obviously, these factors create problems for social change understood as "human engineering."

The first step, then, is not to dismantle or reorganize or rationalize a traditional setting, but to effect change by adding on to the tradition.[8] This is an ancient practice. When Jesus says that he has not come to abolish the law (Matt. 5:17), but to fulfill it, he illustrates this practice. Paul uses this same practice in relation to his struggle with the law. He does not suggest that the law is worthless and to be overthrown. Indeed, we are not to sin all the more that grace might abound (Rom. 6:15). He reminds us: "the law is holy, and the commandment is holy and just and good" (Rom. 7:12). In each of these cases Jesus and Paul were dealing with traditions that would make most of our communal challenges seem mild by comparison, but these are the ways a tradition grows and develops.

A friend of mine once pastored a very traditional and oral

church that had a long-active youth group whose attendance had dropped down to only a half-dozen teens. He wanted the church to have a more active ministry with youth and he also had recognized the genuine need for sex education among teens in the community. Wanting very much to begin such a program, he knew that "sex education" would draw intense resistance. He decided instead to spend a good deal of time with the youth and to visit the parents sharing his interest in youth ministry. After a couple of months he suggested to the youth that it might be good to spend three sessions on sex education, having previously made this clear to the parents and indicating his concern about the need for a Christian approach to this issue. The three sessions lasted three months and the youth group grew to an attendance of more than fifty in a church of just over 200 members. The people of the church could not have been more pleased with the youth group, and those who had expressed concern with this "talking about sex in church" were won over by the renewed interest of the teens. Adding sex education to a tradition of the church had worked very well, and the youth group became an enduring part of the ministry of that congregation.

Originality and Feeding Tradition into New Situations

A second form of doing indigenous social change in oral and traditional settings has to do with the use of the tradition itself, but in new ways and in relation to new circumstances.[9] Originality draws on the tradition, but does so in a departure from the past in order to meet new challenges.

Such an approach to change is often seen as extremely limiting. Too many options are closed off, according to this view, but such a conclusion fails to see how rich tradition is. It is like a deep pool under a large tree: you can find almost anything there.

Thus, it is important to learn the story of a people and to know the tradition. To be without the story is to be like a carpenter without tools. To be without a passion for the tradition is to be like a carpenter without a love of building. It must be said, however, it is a large enterprise to learn the story of a traditional/oral people. Not only is the story complex and manifold, but it is also extremely hard to understand. The notion that traditional/oral people are simple is stupid. One reason for such a view may be that professionals take their theories into these settings and impose them on people, "accounting" for their lives through Meyers-Briggs, Jungian archetypes, family systems theory, functionalism, pop psychology, recovery movements, abuse theories, demographic analysis, or voyeuristic lifestyle descriptions like mine!

Clergy and other professionals cannot learn the tradition without listening to the stories, learning the relationships, and being around long enough to intuit the tacitly known. Stories cannot be reduced to something else. The story means what it says. It does not *have* a point; it *is* the point. Communal relationships are labyrinthine and require membership in the community to begin to understand. Perhaps even more difficult are the tacit understandings and the implicit, informal arrangements and agreements that characterize traditional/oral life. No wonder proverbs embody so much more meaning than their literal expressions!

Still, the pastor who commits to such an apprenticeship will find rich opportunities for ministry. Such ministry will not need to fear new challenges and will be equipped to effect indigenous change and to bring local tradition to bear in original ways to address emerging issues.

Some years ago a United Methodist Church in rural America, made up of traditional/oral people, was informed by the bishop that a woman pastor would be appointed there in two months time. The first response of the congregation was that they would not accept her. They had never had a woman pastor and they were not going to have one now. The bishop held his ground, however, and their second response was that if she came, there would be no one there when she preached. (I'm not sure the bishop ever answered this threat.)

The present pastor of the church was committed to women in ministry and wanted to see his successor's time there be effective. He also knew that what happened after he left a church was a testimony about how well his own ministry had gone. He went to work. Having been there for six years, he knew something about the church and its community and had a solid grasp of how that little church worked. Already he had planned to do his last sermon on the history of the congregation and its contributions to

Christ's work. He also wanted this event to be a new launch forward into the future, setting the stage for his successor. His research on the sermon, which had already begun, now took off in earnest. He read every thing about the church he could find. Visits to city hall and the county courthouse broadened his understanding of the church and its community.

He got lucky—or was it providence?—and discovered that the church had commissioned a missionary to serve in Korea in 1910. *She* worked there for thirty years and then, in the early fifties, returned to the community where she later died. In Korea she taught in a mission school and *on Sundays preached for thirty years in one of the mission churches*. Even more, she still had a great-nephew and a great-niece active in the congregation! The pastor did not regale the church members with charges of hypocrisy. He simply told a few people about what he had found, beginning with the great-nephew and great-niece. They informed him that she was one of the real saints of that church and that people used to tell stories about her all the time. When they told him she had been a preacher, too, in addition to her other responsibilities, his response was simply: "Well, I'll be!"

His inquiries about her, including his intention to remember her in his farewell sermon, began a feast of stories from the old timers re-membering her into the tradition. By the time of the pastor's farewell a transformation had occurred, and the people were enthusuastic about their new pastor to come: "We have a woman coming to be our new preacher; it's a great part of our tradition."

These, then, are basic approaches to social change among traditional, oral people, but, taken alone, they are not enough. Social change will be effected not only in relation to tradition but also in the practices that are indigenous to such people. These will be the focus of the next chapter as we continue to examine social change.

5

Tradition and Practices: Doing Indigenous Social Change

In the previous chapter I suggested approaches to change indigenous to traditional/oral people. Such approaches are traditional practices themselves, but these need to take into account a great range of life-ways that go well beyond approaches that are specifically focused on change. Ministry with traditional/oral people will require the incorporation of change strategies within the communal practices that constitute their lives. This is the task immediately before us. To begin, I need to report a basic change in my own thought and practice in this regard.

For twenty-six years I have taught a course on social change at Saint Paul School of Theology. During that time I have been very much informed by the theory-and-praxis method. This method, of course, has been very important in liberation theology and has shaped the views of many people who work in social change, both as activists and as students of the art.

Stories of traditional change and deeper research into traditional/oral people, however, have led me to shift my view about whether the theory-and-praxis approach is appropriate in a traditional/oral context. Let me describe the theory-and-praxis approach first and then move to my concern. This approach to change begins in praxis: in concrete, material activity. For example, if one were dealing with sharecroppers, one would begin with the concrete activity of the work they do and with the lived reality of their lives. One would focus on the hard work they do, the importance of the crop they raise, and the fact they have so little to show for it. This method, then, involves two phases. The first is that of the practice itself (picking cotton, working long hours, living without some basic necessities) and the second, the reflective moment, stepping back to examine the practice critically and theoretically. This process involves a consciousness-raising among workers who ask questions about their practice to find out why they work so hard and have so little when so much is produced and so much profit is made. Norman Thomas, the six-time Socialist Party candidate for president in the first half of this century, once asked a group of black sharecroppers why they worked so hard to pick cotton, but had no cotton underwear themselves. Such questions are the beginnings of a critical analysis of the practices of exploitation and oppression.

In its focus on theory and practice, liberation theology is indebted to Karl Marx. The great strength of Marxian thought is its concern about the separation of ideas and the social realities of the political economy. This gulf must be bridged. Marx knew that simply exposing contradictions in a society was not enough. A revolutionary movement required workers to move on to bring about a solution. Praxis, then, is a dialectic of practice and critical reflection, with changes in both occurring through the use of the dialectic: the practice gives rise to critical reflection and critical reflection changes the practice which in turn raises new questions for critical attention.

Tradition and Practices, Not Theory-and-Praxis

One of the most serious problems in Marxian thought, in regard to working people, the poor, and the oppressed, is that they themselves don't do theory. Critical reflection, as proposed by Marx, is not indigenous activity. To be sure, the leaders of labor unions and other worker organizations can and do, but most workers do not.

It gets worse. Marx saw capitalism playing a crucial role in the movement toward communist society. The traditional ties of feudalism had to be broken. Traditional ties would be replaced by class relations. The wrongs the workers experienced would be so universal in character that the particularities of their lives would be overcome. For Marx, this was a crucial step in the move toward revolution. The problem with this view was that it was not true.

Marx was an Enlightenment thinker and a fundamental fault of Enlightenment thinkers is that they really believe they are capable of universal knowledge, a problem shared by both Adam Smith and Karl Marx. As such, they believe they can transcend tradition and fail to see that their own thought has a social location and is historically conditioned. They typically disdain tradition because they do not understand how much their thought depends upon a tradition of its own.

Marx, in fact, hated tradition and for that reason had a very low view of peasants. In one classic statement he writes of the French peasants:

> The symbol that expressed their entry into the revolutionary movement, clumsily cunning, knavishly naive, doltishly sublime, a calculated superstition, a pathetic burlesque, a cleverly stupid anachronism, a world-historic piece of buffoonery, and an undecipherable hieroglyphic for the understanding of the civilized—this symbol bore the unmistakable features of the class that represents barbarism within civilization.[1]

In his work Marx failed to see three things. First, not only are peasants oral and traditional, but so are workers, and, as we shall see, class realities get expressed in traditional/oral forms, though these forms change as I have suggested. Second, as indicated above, Marx did not understand that workers are noncritical and that the formulation of theory and practice, while useful in some settings, was simply alien to people who think in stories, proverbs, and relationships. Third, his focus on theory-and-praxis missed the characteristics far more indigenous to the poor and oppressed. With traditional people change is effected in a very different way. For these reasons I believe that liberation theology will be far more effective with traditional people with a switch in focus from theory-and-praxis to tradition and practices.

Practices with Potential for Change

Traditional/oral people do change. I have already indicated the roles of tradition as authority and as resistance and have suggested that traditional groups change by add-on and by bringing to new challenges the resources of the tradition in original ways.

We need now to examine the relation between tradition and traditional practices. In this connection I cannot help but think again of the Gospel of John and that phrase about the Word "pitching tent"—which is a practice—with us (1:14). It is the informing image of what follows. In the incarnation the Word seems to seek out the practices of a people to discover the most effective way to be present, to dwell, and to live with them.

Please understand, these few ideas will not provide a full range of the practices of traditional people. Rather, I hope some depiction of their practices, like other characterizations in this book, will deepen the mystery of oral and traditional people, because it is crucial that we see the profound mystery in their lives. I believe our only hope of understanding will come through a more substantive sense of their otherness. To put it metaphorically: if we do not see them as mysterious, we have no chance of hearing their music. So these suggestions are meant to respect this mystery and to begin the practices of a ministry of social change that will find direction that would not be available to literate-culture practices alone.

What, then, are the practices of traditional and oral people that relate to social change? How can these be discovered in order to pitch tent in an identification with them and practice a ministry of social change that takes them with the utmost seriousness? Here I want to examine six basic practices and their relation to tradition as a direction for indigenous social change.

Storytelling

The first of these has to do with storytelling itself. No more radical activity exists. No amount of discourse can do with traditional and oral people what the concrete, lived stories of ordinary people can accomplish against the organized greed of a system devoted to the bottom line practice of profit at any cost.

No sophistication of theory can assault racism as strongly as the telling of an event that brings full-blown empathy to bear on a practice, empathy that can alter discrimination and the organization of hate. Nowhere in the searing indictments of feminist thought is found a power to match that of the stories of women caught at the bottom of all the hierarchies. The central role of stories needs to be understood by Christians if for no other reason than their place in the teaching of Jesus. It is interesting that the one who pitched tent in John came telling stories in Matthew, Mark, and Luke.

I am deeply concerned about heterosexism and its devastation of gay and lesbian persons in this society. It is clear to me that literate approaches will not touch the people we need to deal with here. But stories can. I remember being present when a friend of mine did a workshop on homosexuality with a group of church persons who were, for the most part, traditional/oral. Chaos ensued, almost from her opening line. It was clear that no presentation would be made by her in that tumultuous setting.

A man in his mid-thirties attempted to get the floor by shouting, "I wonder if I could give a testimony here!" Having used the magic word of "testimony" the crowd turned to hear him. He told this story:

> I was married with children when I finally had to tell my wife that I was gay and could no longer live a lie. Soon, I went to tell my parents. Sitting with them in their living room where I had grown up, I told them that I had been gay from the time I was aware of such things, and that I had to be honest with them because I loved them. When I finished my father went to the closet and took a revolver and a box of cartridges from the top shelf, loaded the gun, walked over and placed it on the lamp table by my chair, and said to my mother: "Come, dear, let's give our son some time by himself." With that they left the room.

It is not my point that everyone in the room was suddenly changed by that testimony—even stories are not panaceas—but the conversation in that workshop changed. There was much more light than heat from that moment on. Similar points could be made of the use of proverbs and thinking in relationships, but we must go on.

Gatherings

A second practice is that of gatherings. As I said earlier, traditional/oral people are far more gather-oriented than goal-oriented. We have known, at least since Emile Durkheim, that if people get together in close physical proximity, focus their attention on a common object, and participate in exercises that arouse emotion, then bonding occurs.[2] Gatherings are the stuff of traditional practices. Many churches are virtually made up of gatherings. The church school classes, the committee meetings, worship, socials, women's and men's meetings, the turkey suppers, and cemetery clean-up days are far more like gatherings than some of the names suggest.

There is hardly a better way to address a community issue than through a gathering. Community organizations across this country know how effective socials, parties, celebrations, festivals, holidays, and feasts are in doing the work of organizing itself.

I remember participating in a training program some years ago with a group of recent college graduates volunteering for mission service at subsistence wages. We went to Franconia, New Hampshire, to see a church that had structured itself on a community organization model and had developed a wood co-operative to offset sharply rising fuel oil prices. I had told the pastor that we wanted to see the wood cooperative and that we wanted to talk with a "panel" of the church people about the work of the congregation.

To "see" the wood cooperative he put the fifty of us to work loading trucks with firewood. It was fun and everyone captured something of the enthusiasm that had seemed contagious in the community. After a hard afternoon's work we returned to the church to discover that the laity were bringing food for a large church supper. The pastor had also asked our students with guitars and singing talent to be ready to lead a hootenanny that evening. As I became agenda anxious about the "panel," he assured me it would be okay.

Following the hootenanny the film of the 250th anniversary of Franconia was shown. It was an awful film. It began with an airplane flying through the mountains of New Hampshire while some perfectly inappropriate and bad "classical" music played in the background. To make matters worse, the projector wasn't working properly, and the film jerked convulsively every few seconds. It went: "dah, dah, de, dah, dah—shudder, shudder—dah, dah, de, dah, dah—shudder, shudder."

By now I was covering my mouth with my hand for fear that my face would reveal how bad I thought the film was. When the credits, airplane, and "classical" music ended, the film began with a pitched, jawbone-to-jawbone, argument between the antique car dealer and the head of the local Veterans of Foreign Wars. The former had been promised he could lead the celebratory parade with his 1897 Oldsmobile and the latter had been told the VFW could lead it with the American flag.

I thought to myself, while hypocritically appearing to enjoy the film, that this was the worst film I had ever seen in my life. About that time the fifty-six-year-old church member sitting next to me drew his arm back, belted me on the shoulder and shouted loud enough for everyone to hear: "Hey, ain't that the hokiest damn film you ever saw!" The whole place erupted in boisterous laughter. From that point on everyone cackled all through the rest of the film and had an uproarious time.

When it ended, an eighty-one-year-old woman who was the town historian of Franconia stood up and, in a carefully choreographed, graceful use of moving arms, dramatic voice inflection, and stirring tone, told us the history of Franconia in about six or seven minutes. It was charming and just right. She was quite simply beautiful.

Well, we never had our panel. There was no description of the church's "program." Yet I left there knowing what they did and how they embodied their corporate lives in these gatherings. I left, too, feeling—true to Durkheim's insight—that I had been strangely bonded to that church.

The Giving and Receiving of Gifts

Perhaps no practice is more important among traditional/oral people than the giving and receiving of gifts. I have seen pastors go into communities determined to be their own persons and to do their own thing and, in the process, violate the reciprocity of giving and receiving indigenous to the community and convey almost immediately that they were clearly alien to the people of the community and intend to remain so.

If one intends to do ministry among traditional/oral people, if one wants to do change there, an understanding of gift exchange is utterly necessary. It is a pervasive practice among oral
and traditional people. The problem for most of us career professionals is that we have become so individualistic, so rational, and
so efficiency-oriented that we fail to see that other people operate on a completely different basis.

One pastor went into a traditional/oral community attempting to establish his own job description, a sixty-hour work
week—which seemed highly reasonable to him—and set office
hours. He was there a year. He so completely attempted to develop a professional description of his work among the people
that he was oblivious to the offerings of gifts, and opportunities
to give in return, and lost countless chances to be a part of the
people, to pitch tent, if you will. The truth of the matter, too, is
that had he worked through the practices of gift exchange, he
probably could have done most of the things he wanted to do,
only in a radically different style.

Anthony Gittins has done a fine review of the anthropolog-
ical literature on gift exchange in his highly readable book *Gifts
and Strangers*. He points out that gift giving and gift exchange
has a "grammar." It is "rule governed" and is "patterned behavior embodying clear moral values." Using the studies of Marcel
Mauss, Gittins distinguishes, but does not separate, "pure economic behavior" from "institutionalized gift exchange." In tradi-
tional/oral societies both are found on "a continuum of behavior
which includes and merges" them both.[3]

Gift exchanges are part of a wider context. They are endemic
to the web of relationships of traditional/oral people and are
often expressive of enduring and reciprocal moral bonds. In such
settings one has an obligation to give, to receive, and to repay.

Gittins, of course, is aware that gift exchange can be
abused, can become a form of power and control, and can place
people in servitude. People living in marginal circumstances
need to be especially aware of these abuses. At the same time,
these possibilities make it no less important to be able to "speak"
the language and know the "grammar" of gift exchange. Moreover, one should not be so preoccupied with the abuses that one
fails to see the enormous bonding and the coping and survival

techniques worked out through the giving and receiving of gifts. It is a well-known observation that people on welfare will often share money, even the little they receive, when they get it. Part of the reason, at least, is that they know it is only a matter of time before they will need help themselves, and this kind of initiation of reciprocity helps to insure the bonding necessary to continue to make it.

Clergy and lay leadership will do well to watch carefully the "rituals" of gift exchange in a community to see how they work, what is regarded as a gift, what constitutes a payback, and, hence, what commensurate gifts are. I had a friend some years ago who drove a truck for a living. He could buy used plywood for a low price. I would then buy it from him for some of my amateur work projects. He made a profit, but it was clearly worth it to me. This was an economic transaction. On another occasion I was unable to fix a car of mine, being without even amateur skills in auto repair. He worked hours on it without any compensation. This was a gift, although I knew it involved an obligation on my part. I later conducted his wedding and made myself available whenever he needed, as he said, to "air out" some of his troubles.

In most traditional settings the gifts that clergy are asked to provide in the context of the United States are mainly the duties of calling, of hospital visitation, of presence, of listening, and of laughing and crying with people through the good and hard times. When one goes to a traditional setting to do ministry, it helps to listen to what a previous pastor did that endeared him or her to the people. Lurking in the midst of these stories are hints and instruction on the rituals of gift exchange. One will find clarification about what the appropriate gifts and reciprocity are.

Argue, Fuss, Gripe, Complain, Moan, and Gossip

Fourth, I have said that traditional/oral people do not do critique, but this does not mean they do not have practices that call things into question. What they do instead is argue, fuss, gripe, complain, moan, and gossip. Because of our literate preoccupation with critique, we have failed to participate in these arts of resistance and subversion, judgment and discernment. These arts are capable of the most devastating treatment of issues close to the lived realities of traditional people. The task is not so much to teach oral and traditional people theoretical critique as it is to develop our own powers to participate in practices indigenous to these people. Arguments, fusses, gripes, complaints, and moaning can take on sharp focus and be directed at true problems. Moreover, they can embody the concrete experience of the issue for traditional people in a way that theoretical discourse cannot.

Gossip is often attacked by preachers and others. It can, of course, be destructive, but it also serves quite positive purposes. Gossip can be a way to check out events going on and can be an important dynamic in community building. The point is not to eliminate gossip—an unlikely possibility—but to encourage its positive use. The word "gossip" is a combination of "god" and "sib" and originally comes from the kinds of conversations occurring at extended family gatherings like religious ceremonies, weddings, and funerals. Sister Gertrude Maley, M.M. observes that "Godsib," as such, is holy and appropriate talk. Moreover, in its constructive uses gossip can serve to fight destructive rumors by communicating more accurate information.[4]

Solidarities and Factional Conflict

Fifth, no examination of traditional practices would be complete without a consideration of the place of solidarities and factional conflict.[5] In the United States, for example, class realities tend to be expressed in solidarities. People in the United States are uncomfortable with the whole idea of class. They do not typically like to talk about it. But social class is very real and usually takes its most organized form, in this society, in a range of solidarities: churches, barber shops and beauty salons, veterans organizations, sports teams, bowling leagues, motorcycle clubs, tractor pulls, auto racing, Wednesday night bingo, tole painting, craft classes, social and recreational activities, and in saloons and local bar life. When Garth Brooks came out with his hit country song,"Friends in Low Places," it had an incredible impact in the largest honky-tonk in Kansas City. The dance floor was jammed and the rest of the crowd gathered around the people dancing the two-step and sang along with the chorus of "Friends in Low Places." I have seldom seen a greater expression of "class consciousness" in my life.

I remember one college that had difficulty in keeping ethnic faculty members because of negative community responses in the small town where the school was located. Someone came up with the idea that the president of the college should hold receptions for groups like the barkeepers union, veterans organizations, the country music bands of the area, and so on, to solicit their help in making the community more hospitable to ethnic newcomers. Approaches like these would pay off well, not only in helping the college to keep valued faculty, but in helping create a deeper working relationship between the college and people they seldom connect with.

One can hardly mention solidarities without addressing the place of factions and factional conflict. Many pastors have served churches riven by deep factional conflicts and will not be surprised or relieved to hear these are traditional practices, much less that I want to encourage them! But take a closer look. Hamza Alavi maintains that factions are the pervasive form of political interaction in the villages he has studied. Emerging during times of conflict, they frequently deal with uses of power in the public arena. Factions cut across the horizontal solidarities of family, caste, and class and, by that fact, can provide alternative organizing centers to them.[6]

I am intrigued by the National Rifle Association, although I disagree with them on just about everything. Yet, the NRA seems to know how to take advantage of factional conflict. Its members come from almost every class and represent a wide spectrum of political groups, veterans organizations, hunting and fishing enthusiasts, some environmentalists, and many others. It has the capacity to raise sharp factional opposition when conflict arises around gun issues.

Those on the other end of the political spectrum have missed an opportunity for effective action when they have not been adept at the use of such traditional practices. Moreover, by not addressing contemporary issues in both traditional forms and in terms of their values and interests, we leave such work for the right-wing extremists who are more than ready to do so, but who do so in order to advance agendas at odds with many of the genuine claims of traditional/oral people.

I realize that factional conflict can be risky business in the local church, and dangerous to play around with. My point, however, is that it exists. It will be best dealt with through traditional means that help people think in communal relationships, tell the stories, offer the plumb-line proverbs, and claim a solidarity in Christ that enables a community to work with factional strife but not be overcome by it.

At the very least, traditional change will work with the rhythms of solidarities and factions since both are pervasive forms of communal life. These do not eradicate the overriding politics of class, but they do complicate it. While solidarities often embody class realities, factions cut across them. This is another reason why Marxists who focus exclusively on class factors bring an inadequate analysis and a truncated approach to social change.

Politics as Morality

A final practice we can examine relates to the fact that a lot of traditional people do not participate in politics. The reasons for this are not altogether clear. Those who are most conservatively religious often feel that politics is "of the world" and involves too much compromise.

With most traditionally oral people politics is too far removed from their lifeways; it is something apart from what they typically do. They are too often not organized in their workaday lives in forms that are politically effective. Moreover, their tactics of resistance are not of the kind that promote initiative in political action. Besides, politics can be scary business if one is put in a setting that requires rhetoric and a form of discourse alien to one's own approach to issues.

These are but a sampling of the reasons, but they at least suggest why political activity by oral and traditional people is such hard going at times. In fairness, it needs also to be said that most Americans do not involve themselves in politics. I once met a man who had a bumper sticker on his car that said "I did not vote for him." This message suggested his displeasure with a current holder of the elective office of President. Upon inquiring whom he did vote for, I discovered he did not vote at all!

For oral and traditional people political action takes the form of politics as morality. This is especially true of those who are deeply committed to their religion. Involvement beyond conventional ways of voting and electoral politics requires a feeling on their part that something is desperately wrong in a moral sense.[7] This concern will engage them far more actively than issues on other subjects. This trait reflects the conflict between modernity and tradition, on the one hand, and the commitment to family, neighborhood, and other primary groups, on the other. That is, they will not be moved by appeals for "progress and development." They are the socio-moral conservatives. (Note well, they are not political conservatives committed to laissez-faire economics.) They will be stirred to action by events involving their families, their communities, and their faith. This characteristic also has to do with the way an issue touches the empathic core and moral heart of their lives. Their sporadic involvement in politics is not reducible to other non-moral issues alone, but arises from an intrinsically moral sensibility as well.

The country music song, "Harper Valley P.T.A.," represents politics as morality in a clear and unambiguous way. With words and music by Tom T. Hall it has an authoritative source because Hall is noted as one of the great storytellers of country music and his song, recorded by Jeannie C. Riley, topped the charts in 1968 and has remained popular ever since.[8]

The song is about the story of a widow who receives a letter from the secretary of the Harper Valley P.T.A. The letter states that the widow wears her dresses much too short, drinks and runs around with the wrong crowd, and lives on the wild side of life in ways unfit for raising her little girl. As the narrator of the story, her daughter describes in specific detail her mother going to the next meeting and "socking it" to the members of the P.T.A. Her mother describes the moral failures of each board member and then accuses them individually and collectively of being hypocrites of the first order. It seems clear that the mother had never attended a board meeting before or any other political event, for that matter, and probably never would again, but the moral criticism of her, by those guilty of shenanigans that made her own look mild in comparison, was more than she could take.

Politics as morality is not an unmixed blessing, of course. It can be a source of fanaticism and it can render a relative political position absolutistic in ways which are inattentive to those with other equally pressing moral concerns. It can give one the sense that the opposition is constituted of the enemies of God and can consign them, not only to hell, but to a subhuman status as well.

At the same time, moral and political excesses are not the special province of traditional and oral people, and the rooting of their politics in moral concerns means that they can be approached in terms of the empathic core and from an indigenous practice of morality that has enormous possibilities for ethical compassion and conduct. In politics, as in morality, we have the joining of traditional morality and traditional social change. That these bring risk and potential for abuse no more lessens their centrality and constructive potential than life itself, known to possess no little peril and torment of its own.

In sum, these factors are but a few illustrations of the ways traditional and oral people deal with social change. These, along with a growing but selective list, offer an array of indigenous practices for a contextual ministry:

> thinking in stories, proverbs and relationships,
> memorization,
> mentoring and apprenticeship,
> the focus on concrete and practical life,
> empathic and relational morality,
> the use of tradition and traditional authority,
> resistance and subversion,
> gatherings,
> arguing, fussing, complaining, and gossiping,
> solidarities,
> factions and factional conflicts.

While each of these practices is related to faith and religious commitment, I have not yet given this relation the kind of explicit consideration it deserves. We will examine this in the next chapter.

6

A Faith Language of the Heart: Believing and Feeling with Traditional/Oral People

For over twenty years Sam Mann, a white Alabaman, has been the pastor of Saint Mark's Church, an African-American congregation in the central city of Kansas City, Missouri. Sam tells the story of one of his early sermons there. He preached, as he says, on his Christology, and believes that he did it well in terms of representing the theological thought of the church. His professors from seminary, he felt, would have been pleased. Following the service, however, he was confronted by Mrs. Nichols, a seventy-eight-year-old matriarch of the church, who grabbed him by the sleeve of his robe with one hand and pointed in his face with the other. Sam offers that whenever a seventy-eight-year-old woman who weighs a hundred pounds gets you by the robe sleeve, you have been had. As she reprovingly waved her finger under his nose, she said to him in measured terms:

"Reverend Mann, Reverend Mann, I did not come to this church to hear what somebody else said *about* Jesus. I came to hear what *Jesus* said to *you!*"

Her comment captures what this concluding chapter attempts to understand. Many pastors will tell you that the theology they learned in seminary, no matter how valuable it is, has to be reworked in order to communicate with people who are oral and traditional. Among the reasons are those that relate to the distinctions between literate approaches and more oral ones.

Relational Thought and Conceptual Thought

Perhaps the most important distinction is the one between relational thought and conceptual thought. In Mrs. Nichols's comment we see this clearly. Conceptual thought is talking *about* Jesus, it is not listening *to Jesus*. To be sure, most theologians would break out in a cold sweat claiming to represent what Jesus said to them, but their discomfort reflects the difference in what is being claimed. Strictly speaking, theology is conceptual. It attempts to state exactly, in highly nuanced language, an understanding of Christ that is responsive to scripture, the tradition of the church, the canons of reason, and contemporary experience, on the one hand, and their meaning for the church today, on the other. In contrast, Mrs. Nichols seems to want Sam to talk about his relation to Jesus, about his time in prayer, and his thoughts when he is with Jesus. These are two very different languages that are tied up with very different activities. Fortunately, the languages can and do often overlap, at least in the theologians it has been my pleasure to know well.

A Christian theologian is attempting to represent the life and thought of the church while the people of faith address the challenges of the day. The theologian will often be attempting to speak to more than one situation, although trying to speak across cultures is dangerous, if not sometimes lethal, work. Theological activity requires conceptualization, even when it takes narrative and metaphor with the utmost seriousness.

Moreover, it is not finally necessary to separate concepts and relationships. Mrs. Nichols does a kind of conceptual work of her own. She seems to want Sam to be able to summarize his life with Jesus. After all, even in a long sermon he cannot report everything that has happened between Christ and him. This effort certainly involves a type of conceptualization that is considerably relieved by Sam's telling the most important stories that embody his life with Jesus.

The problem with conceptualization is that it so often leads to what the philosopher Wittgenstein called the "craving for generality."[1] It consumes the particular in a colonial imposition of conceptual categories, which distorts the particular and local into alien abstractions. I might add that this is the error I fear most about my work here.

Still, the distinction between, not the separation of, concept and relationship is important. Traditional and oral people will talk about the faith in terms of relationships. We have seen the importance of this in oral life-ways, in traditional morality, and in social change. We should be surprised if it did not prove to be so here in the language of faith as well.

Traditional/oral people make a sharp distinction between theories about God and "actually knowing the Lord." Their concern is not with their view of God but their relationship to God. They are interested, not in Christology, but in Christ; not in pneumatology, but in the Spirit. Conceptual thought about God "distances" oral people from God. It cuts them off from the power of God so essential to face the hard edges of a recalcitrant world that requires day-to-day struggle.

Tacit Understanding

A faith language of the heart will, more often than not, be tacitly understood. We have seen how traditional/oral people know things they cannot say, feel things they cannot express in words (at least not the words of discourse) and believe things they cannot explain. When it comes to faith there really are sighs too deep for words.[2]

First, a faith language of the heart is an expressive communication. It deals with life at several levels. For one, it attempts to convey feeling by people who are not that introspective—in the sense that they are not trying to nuance the subtleties and the shadings of these inner dynamics into conceptual frameworks. Further, as we have seen, stories, proverbs, and relationship thinking are more implicit and not usually devoted to theoretical exactions. Even more basic, life is deeper than logic, and religion as a way of life, as Robert Schreiter has so helpfully said, is more than religion as a view of life.[3] Since oral people are not so discursively oriented, their language points toward realities they do not even need to name explicitly. In talking about such they typically rely on that well-worn, but exceedingly worthy, phrase so

existentially wrought from a world of implicit mysteries and explicit living: "You know what I mean?"

Second, tacit understanding is intimately related to sound,
and I mean sound itself. Chukwulozie Anyanwu reports that, in
an African understanding, sound is the model of reality and the
criterion of truth. It is the model of music, creativity, intelligibility, and rationality. Sound can explain, predict, and control
events. It can induce attitudes and indicate certain ways of behavior. Life itself is known aesthetically through sound, dance,
art, and music. Indeed, sound can shape, increase, or decrease
the power of the Life Force.[4]

We were discussing Anyanwu's views in class one day
when Elijah Nagbe, a visiting student from Liberia, spoke up
and affirmed what Anyanwu had said. "When I left Liberia, my
people told me not to come back preaching like an American."
When asked what that meant, he went on to explain that "to
preach in my country requires that one make the right sound.
Sound can either bring the Spirit or drive the Spirit away. My
people wanted to make sure that I did not lose my capacity to
do this."

Placing such emphasis upon sound, as such, is not really
strange to the United States. I have heard teenagers, sharply at-
tuned to the electronic orality of rock music, move down the
street listening to a boom box and saying to themselves, "That's
real, that's real, man!" More to the point, I have reflected on this
in terms of preaching in at least some oral congregations in the
United States. The full round tones, the "holy" sound of some
preaching is so integral to the preaching in these churches that,
without it, one simply is not preaching. When I studied homilet-
ics, "the ministerial tone" was excoriated and treated with
amusement and derisive laughter. Looking back, my suspicion is
that we were being prepared for ministry with literate congregations. In an oral setting the round tones we derided are the very
stuff out of which the Spirit comes. In such congregations the
modulated, conversational speaking styles more typical of the
professional churches of the middle class are "not spiritual" and,
as one woman said, "too humdrum."

Third, tacit understanding uses encoded language. The
words mean more than they say. It is not enough to listen to

them in a literal fashion alone. One must "look beneath" what is spoken in order to understand what is actually being said. I have a friend who is a folk theologian. Our conversations inevitably turn "theological." In his own folk theology I am often amazed at the way he works through questions of faith. He will tell a story about TV evangelists, about how their use of religion is wrong, and then come around to some assertion that almost knocks me off my chair. One day he had been on a tear about the immoralities and exploitative abuses of one evangelist in particular. At the end of one of these meandering monologues of stories and implicit silences he said: "That guy could count his balls twice and come up with a different number both times."

From the standpoint of a linear and a literal development of his comments, the line does not make sense. He is talking about unethical and unfaithful conduct, yet his comment is about the man's inability to "count." But not really. His below-the-belt punch line is a proverbial saying that speaks to one's very basic ability to live and operate in the world even on an elementary basis. The immoral and faithless behavior of the TV evangelist raises issues about being in the world that surpass more specialized interests in religion and ethics as such. His comment is profoundly theological because it actually calls into question the evangelist's capacity to connect with anything at all. If he cannot count his balls he is utterly out of touch—he really is lost.

Survival and Coping; Identity and Belonging; Trust and Assurance

The activities of oral and traditional people are different from those of the theologians. Most of them are not affluent, and many are poor. Although millions of people in the United States are illiterate, most traditional people are not, but they are *traditionally oral.* As we have seen, they think in proverb, story, and relationships. We now need to see more explicitly how this works in terms of faith.

Traditional/oral people approach faith in terms of survival and coping far more than they do in terms of systematic understanding and coherence. Assurance and trust are much more central to their faith than are discourse and explanation.

Belonging and identity take precedence over comprehension and consistency of argument. Each of these needs further development.

It is easy to underestimate the power religious faith has for people who face the wearisome, unending task of "making it through the night" and then the day. Coping with incessant demands that come to those for whom the money and the wherewithal are always short tries the human spirit in a way that depletes the nerves and exhausts the will. Knowing that tomorrow will not be different and the basic outlines of one's life will not change, knowing that this is the way things are, and that no relief resides in this world: this is an ecology of futility and despair.

Alasdair MacIntyre says that real courage is when one sees the pattern of one's life and then has the courage to face it and live it out.[5] This courage for most traditional/oral people comes through a faith that sustains one's capacity to cope and survive beyond any empirical justification. The easy retort, one without much thick description, is that theirs is a narcotic religion. Mind you, it is a faith that gets people up in the morning, that keeps them keeping on, that sustains them through death and life, and that even gives voice to some to sing: "It's another day's journey and I'm glad about it." It is a faith that holds uncanny compassion and capacity for people who manage to give what they have when they have so little. It is obscene to relegate such human spirituality to the status of an opiate. Note that such a charge typically comes from people who are quite clear that they know what ultimate reality is, or, perhaps more importantly for them, what it is not.

The issue, of course, is not only economic. Not all traditional people have hard economic lives. For some the coping and survival come in response to other kinds of challenge. I remember once in class I was making fun of the song "In the Garden." Not only did I parody its lyrics as hopelessly individualistic, privatistic, and full of escapist spirituality, but I launched out into singing it in a nasal voice with affront aforethought. I was on a roll until after the class when a thirty-five-year-old woman approached me and told this story.

> Tex, my father started screwing me when I was eleven and he kept it up until I was sixteen and found the strength somehow to

stop it. After every one of those ordeals I would go outside and sing that song to myself: "I go to the garden alone while the dew is still on the roses, and he walks with me and talks with me and he tells me I am his own." Without that song I don't know how I could have survived. Tex, don't . . . you . . . ever . . . ever . . . make fun of that song in my presence again.

Wittgenstein is correct. A word's meaning depends on how it is used. It is also true of hymns. I remember being told that good old hymns are not good and not old. I was so mesmerized by my newly-found sophistication that I did not stop to think about how such music was used by the very people I was raised with and how their experience did not square with this new "critique" I had just heard. I now believe that such a critique came from career people struggling with the individualism of their own lives more than the communal—and not individualistic—coping of the traditional/oral cultures many of them came from. It is one thing to sing "In the Garden" as privatistic sentimentalism and escapist individualism. It is quite another when it sustains the survival of people who struggle to make it one more day.

It is important to understand that the actual words to the hymns do not mean the same thing to all people. There is no unvarying essence these words have, apart from how they are used, and neither professional "cosmopolitanism" nor academic training necessarily fits one to make such Olympian judgments. Parenthetically, I am amazed when I find people who take the scripture seriously without taking it in every case literally, but can make no such distinction with the hymnody. Some who decry biblical fundamentalism have no such qualms about the same kind of literal rigidity with sacred songs.

Does this mean that nothing is ever wrong with the way traditional people use language or songs or beliefs or whatever? Of course not. Mary D. Pellauer reports on her work with victims of sexual abuse about how often the word "God" brings out a punitive strand of language and thought. Clearly, popular expressions of traditional faith have problems.

Yet, Pellauer then goes on to say how important it is to get to people's experience and to hear them as they talk in very ordinary ways. As they then begin to tell about their spirituality,

something more healthful and sound and authentic in terms of
faith begins to happen. One of the most helpful perspectives Pellauer brings, however, is in understanding how complex the ordinary is. She knows how crucial it is to connect with the stories
of people and to do so through the complex ordinariness of their
lives. She is wary of "theories" that account for too much and
that distort the lived lives of the people she knows in her own
work. She says:

> Yes, the ordinariness of the processes, I think, is very important . . . .
> It may be part of my Christian background to look for the extraor-
> dinary in the ordinary, or to see or to form my eyes so as to see
> when the very mundane thing begins to shimmer around the
> edges and to speak values beyond itself, or to point at something
> else, or to begin to glow, even though it's not shiny at all. I'm not
> sure how to talk about that. To look for parables maybe in ordi-
> nary stories . . . .[6]

Approaches like this offer hope for traditional people
through indigenous forms of transformation and change.

Let it be clear, my point is not that traditional oral life and
understanding are a seamless robe of primal, redemptive, and
liberative practices. They are not. The impulse to transformation—basic to Christian faith—is requisite for traditional/oral
people no less than others. What is important is that this transformation not be a transmogrification into bourgeois categories
that are already in enough trouble of their own.

The questioning of traditionally oral language and practices comes best out of a close and caring relationship, working,
as Pellauer says, through the complex ordinariness of their lives.
In such things one must "descend into detail"—as Clifford
Geertz says in characterizing "thick" description.[7] One must also
be aware that most people contend with a conspiracy of taste in
this culture that is pervasive in its imperious dismissal of people
who do not fit its obviously Archimedean savoir-faire.

A faith language of the heart is also one of trust and assurance. Mitchell and Cooper-Lewter find these in what they call
"the core beliefs" of the African-American community. These
core beliefs are "the bedrock attitudes that govern all deliberate

behavior and relationships and also all spontaneous responses to crises."[8] They argue that "the issue is not the correctness of formulation but the adequacy of trust in the Creator, as evidenced by the ability to cope with one's life experiences." Their concern is with what happens to the power of grace when the primary concern of theology is exactness of words rather than "an elaboration of the word that is revered because it gives life, serves needs, and heals minds and bodies by way of a powerful core belief or trust in God."[9]

William B. McClain captures these same characteristics in his preface to *Songs of Zion*, a songbook from the black religious tradition published under the auspices of the United Methodist Church. In writing about the theology expressed in the gospel song, McClain states:

> The gospel song expresses theology. Not the theology of the university, not the formalistic theology or the theology of the seminary, but a *theology of experience*—the theology of a God who sends the sunshine and the rain, the theology of a God who is very much alive and active and who has not forsaken those who are poor and oppressed and unemployed. It is a *theology of imagination*—it grew out of fire shut up in the bones, of words painted on the canvas of the mind. Fear is turned to hope in the sanctuaries and storefronts, and bursts forth in songs of celebration. It is a *theology of grace* that allows the faithful to see the sunshine of His face—even through their tears. Even the words of an ex-slave trader become a song of liberation and an expression of God's amazing grace. It is a *theology of survival* that allows a people to celebrate the ability to continue the journey in spite of the insidious tentacles of racism and oppression and to sing: "It's another day's journey and I'm glad about it."[10]

This language of trust and assurance can be found across a range of traditional and oral people and in different traditions and experiences. Many Anglo-European working people in the United States find it expressed in country music. Someone has suggested that country music is a soap opera put to music. It is hurtin' music, but it also contains hope and a trust and assurance. No matter how bad the loss of lovers, pickups, the farm, the job, the children, country music, at the very least, is hounded with a conviction that life is not supposed to be this way. One does not have to listen long to hear that a brighter day is ahead or that one truly "did see the light."

Finally, it must not be overlooked how much a faith language of the heart is one of identity and belonging. It arises from the people, from common, ordinary, life-engaged people, who struggle with family and work, with home and neighborhood, with church and school, and with the exigencies of a universe out of their control where the very stars ramble and roam. Such an indigenous faith provides an interpretive tradition for engaging and facing the world, and no little part of this functions to provide identity by demarking those who are insiders and those who are not; those who belong and those who do not. These are local people, after all. Such boundaries represent life as one knows it and make sense out of place. True, a boundary mindset can be as narrow, bigoted, myopic, and self-serving as any loyalty that places people beyond the veil of flesh and blood.

It is also true that deep identities and powerful bonds can check anxieties, call into question the arrogance and overreach of the human spirit, and touch and call to life those gutted by passivity and self-loss. We miss the strength and health of a faith language of the heart when we fail to see the life that comes to those who are given a name when before they had no name. The yearning to belong, as much as any elemental dream, takes up residence at the center of the human heart.

Perhaps one example will serve here. I often wonder why traditional/oral people who are not fundamentalists so often defend the literal truth of the Bible. Fundamentalism is far too rationalistic and too ideological for the non-critical tastes of most traditional/oral folk. It finally becomes clear that the issue is not one of fundamentalist commitments but one of traditional loyalties. The Bible is family and home; it is identity and bond. It may not even be read! But it is a basic expression of who they are and to whom they belong. They are not defending some overwrought doctrine of inerrancy; they are defending the Bible.

Does this mean that the Bible cannot be read with attention to "critical" issues? Not at all. Traditional/oral people argue about the Bible all the time. The question is whether the arguments come from a framework that is perceived as loyal or from one viewed as subversive. Do the questions come from a faith language of the heart that grounds its concerns in coping and survival, trust and assurance, and identity and belonging? The problem is one of dealing with the text in indigenous terms. Traditional/oral people are often seen as interested in what is called "devotional" Bible study rather than critical examination. This is not altogether correct because the issue is not only devotional but also one focused on the issues of coping, belonging, and so on.

The point is that scripture, like a host of other matters, will look very different when seen in terms of the indigenous faith lives of people. It is not enough simply to label and dismiss their views as deviant according to some imperialistic and alien "discipline" that consigns them to a hinterland of ignorance and backwoods crudity.

All of this is to say that a faith language of the heart will not be understood apart from the struggle of traditionally oral people to cope and survive, to seek out a faith of trust and assurance, and to claim who they are and to whom they belong. It has a different "logic" and a set of standards all its own. It will fail these standards, as all human aspirations do, in the enduring exactions of everyday claims. But a faith language of the heart *has* "criteria" to determine adequacy. Its "coherence" is measured in the resilience of the people who so believe; its "consistency" in their capacity to cope; its "cogency" in continuing to choose life; its "methodological assumptions" in a bedrock trust in God; its "explanatory power" in the regeneration of human hope; its "discourse" in stories and proverbs of humor and wisdom; its "critical" edge in the fussing, complaints, and gossip about real life relationships; its accountability in tactics of subversion and resistance; its sophistication in the day-by-day savvy it takes to make it to tomorrow; and its sustaining power of "argument" in an assurance that God watches over us because even sparrows fall within the divine purview.

You see, its adequacy is not in a sustained intellectual tour de force, but rather in its capacity to help people through the night and then to get them up in the morning. Everything, even doubt, rests on some kind of trust. Trust of some kind is inevitable. For oral people this trust will not be articulated in the subtleties of theoretical language adequate to the criteria of academic discourse. Rather, the depths of such trust are spoken, and left unsaid, in notions and phrases and silences and sometimes in profane utterance. To speak "the sweet name of Jesus" names a sense, a reality, a trust not finally expressed in words but embodied in a sustained human striving.

Beliefs and Traditional Language Practices

Pitching a tent and living in a tent are practices. In the Gospel of John the original Greek, as we have seen in Chapter 4, uses the pitching of tent as a metaphor for the "dwelling" or "living" of the Word made flesh with us. In our understanding of the incarnation more needs to be done with this enculturation dimension, especially with the idea that the Word not only becomes flesh, but also takes on the practices of a people. More than that, the Word, in pitching a tent, takes on the specific language practices of a particular people. Any expression of the Word in language requires some linguistic practice, and no such practice is universal.

Language as a practice varies greatly across the cultures and subcultures of the world. The concern of this entire book is the practices of traditional/oral people, and this chapter especially emphasizes their language practices in the United States around issues of faith. So far we have looked at what happens when people think about the faith relationally and tacitly. We also examined the ways in which faith gives people the capacity to cope and survive, an identity and belonging, and the trust and assurance to make it through the night.

Still one more thing needs to be done. The focus, so far, has been more on how faith empowers and sustains traditional/oral people. We have not looked as directly at the beliefs themselves in relation to the situations or the contexts in which traditional/oral people live. What is the impact of context on the content of the beliefs they hold? Closely related to this, what is the relationship between the life and thought of the church across history and the specific expressions of traditional and oral people? Much of the criticism of oral and traditional people is done by clergy and theologians. Can any perspective on traditional/oral people be offered to move this set of issues along?

I want to suggest something about the direction we need to

take to gain a more adequate understanding of the beliefs of oral
and traditional people. We need to provide evidence of more authentic expressions of Christian faith among oral and traditional
people, on the one hand, and offer directions for more faithful
understanding where traditional beliefs may be narcotic, or destructive, or otherwise not fully faithful, on the other.

First, something must be said about the inadequacy and the
necessity of words. Words do not have an eternal meaning. In
the study of language we find that words change. In our more
recent experience words vary and mean different things over
even short periods of time. I think particularly of the way in
which "hot" and "cool" have changed in the last fifty years.
Today "cool"—even though its meaning varies—is prized the
way "hot" used to be in terms of something that is "with it"
(though I suspect my use of the term "with it" is now passé).

Words also vary with context. I think of the difference in
meaning of the word "beautiful" when giving expressive utterance to a 250-yard drive on a golf course, on the one hand, and
when whispered in hushed awe at a buttermilk sky and a full
moon on the other. When one crosses cultures and subcultures,
the difference in words, even when they translate to mean
roughly the same thing, can connote even deeper differences.
For example, in a culture where pigs provide many of the functions (in terms of food) that lambs did in biblical times, would
one need to talk about Christ as "the pig of God" rather than
"the lamb of God" in order to convey more adequately a bibli-
cally-informed faith?

Even more, when one addresses the mysteries of this world
and of the gospel, not only does one face the variability and con-
textuality of language, but I doubt that any words are as yet even
adequate in expressing the full meaning of God's good news in
Jesus Christ. What I want to do, then, is suggest what certain beliefs of traditional people mean when understood in context.

To do so I choose three beliefs for illustrative purposes that
are perhaps the bane of existence for many clergy who want to
represent the life and thought of the church more fully. These
three are: being born again, being washed in the blood of the
lamb, and heaven.

Each of these has some biblical and traditional precedent,

of course, and can be part of some more systematic theology. In their typical traditional usage, however, these beliefs can take on implications that daunt the most sensitive pastoral heart.

Born Again

Let me confess at the beginning that a good many "born again" Christians drive me to distraction. My distaste for such expressions of faith led me to re-examine my views in an attempt to understand better, at least, what traditional/oral people mean when they say it. Understanding this phrase is a complex matter. In some cases it is used by drug abusers who see themselves living now in the utterly new life of sobriety. Without the help of God and Alcoholics Anonymous (or Narcotics Anonymous) they simply could not make it. In other cases, it is the language of people who have been living on the wild side of life. Due to a conversion experience they have been able to get some semblance of order in their lives and, perhaps, recover their families and their jobs. To such people to be born again is to live again.

Most traditional/oral people, however, are not drug abusers or hard livers on the wild side of life. For many, being born again is the way one becomes a Christian. The influence of revivalism is still present, and the passage to a faithful life is to be born again. Many traditional/oral people can point to a time when it happened, although the experiences vary and cannot be reduced to one kind. Being born again comes with the territory of being a Christian.

Further, to be born again sets one apart from what the world has to offer. The born-again experience comes from beyond this world. One can understand why it is important to have such a blessing from God in a world where most of one's life is not privileged, much less validated, as in the day-to-day experience of more oral and traditional people. In a literate and post-literate world, traditional orality is not exactly the latest thing.

Still, I do not want to reduce born-again experience to a compensative construction or simply a ritualistic function in an oral culture. It is the name of a decidedly Christian existence. It is usually an alternative to conventional living in the United States, and typically involves much greater commitment to a life in the church. More of one's time is spent in the church, and one's friends and activities are there. It is, if you will, a way of life, really a diversity of ways of life, involving a range of practices not reducible to any simplistic characterizations. It is a way to be faithful to God. Clergy will be better served in their attempts to be in ministry by paying attention to the rich particularity of a people's life than by attributing to them the stereotypes so popular in the wider culture.

Washed in the Blood

Walter Ong reports how agonistic oral cultures are. In its more primal expression, oral thought occurs in a context of struggle. It is often characterized by "verbal tongue lashings," "portrayals of violence," and "gory details." Ong attributes this to the often unyielding and ever-present hardship in life.[11] It should be no secret that such hardship scores the lives of many traditional/oral people today. An agonistic "logic" operates among oral and traditional people. It is a life where everything costs. An agonistic economy is a market of injury for injury. In a world where life costs so much and where commensurability is seen in such harsh equations, the pay-offs, the resolutions, the getting even, and even the redemption will come in the gory coinage of up-against-the-wall commerce.

What I have tried to see is the way such "logic" operates in the indigenous thought of people who are traditionally oral and agonistic. For such folk a faith language must engage this kind of "logic" and address an agonistic "economy." Not to do so is simply to miss a fundamental dimension in their lives.

Therefore, language like "washed in the blood of the lamb" is vitally important to many traditional and oral people. To be sure, they could be correct in this formulation of the atonement, but, in any case, a language that does not engage the world with an understanding of how existentially expensive things are will not connect with the intelligibility of an agonistic people. That God should have to give God's Son in the blood and gore of crucified agony seems decidedly on target. It makes sense in a deep pool of tacit acknowledgement, unexplicated in discourse, but spelled out in lives that know quiet desperation and hardship.

On matters like these I must confess how much I feel the

need for more work with such indigenous expressions. Alien critique will not do. Answers that do not connect with the "thick" particularity of the lives of people will remain irrelevant, except for their colonial capacity to overlay traditional lives with language and ideologies not finally suited for the world in which they live. Here is where indigenous forms of morality, change, and faith are required to find practices of nonviolence that embody peaceable Christian living. Part of the direction resides in indigenous understandings of heaven.

Heaven

This third belief, heaven, may have little or nothing to do with the New Testament teaching of Jesus on the Kingdom or Realm of God. Moreover, I do not want to argue altogether against the observation that it is sometimes used in a narcotic fashion.

What I do want to suggest is that a traditional understanding of heaven can take on a more constructive direction from the perspective of the faith, and that this kind of indigenous grasping of the realities of the gospel is one direction for a contextualized understanding.

Michel de Certeau, in a discussion of the ordinary language of popular culture, writes about a "utopian space in which a possibility, by definition miraculous in nature, was affirmed by religious stories."[12] He describes this in contrast to "the reign of mendacity" where the rich and the police always win and where there is no truth.

His comment led me in a search to understand the use of heaven in traditional and oral language. It is clear that heaven is typically used in sharp contrast to the world as traditional people know it. It is a land where the overwhelming weariness ends, where there is no pain, no death, no weeping, and where things are finally set right. The more I have attempted to sensitize myself to this use of the word heaven, the more I find it becomes key for understanding indigenous faith. Too often we clergy make a sharp distinction between a popular-view heaven and a New Testament-informed understanding of the Commonwealth of God. I now believe this to be a mistake. What is needed is to fill the notion of heaven even more fully with the New Testament images and parables of the Reign. Heaven is, or can be, the expression of indigenous vision, of the way the world is supposed to be. It can be an alternative to the oppression and exploitation of the principalities and powers.

Miguez Bonino makes a distinction between the supernatural screen of traditional religion in Latin America and the subjective screen of Protestantism. The former sees the events of nature like weather, illness, and day-to-day happenings as the work ultimately of superhuman powers, both divine and demonic. The events of life are projected onto a supernatural screen. These supernatural powers direct and control life. Religious practices are then used to influence these powers, to curry their favor, and to avoid their ire. In Protestantism, while the supernatural emphasis is still present, nevertheless the faith is projected on a screen of subjectivity where it is understood in terms of inner states such as "joy," "peace," and "experience."[13] Subjective faith is pervasive in the United States and melded with popular psychology especially. In fact, some religiosity seems little more than a half-wet baptism of popular behavioral science, "I'm OK, you're OK, and it's OK," in a combination of cheap grace and even less expensive psychology.

Yet, the supernatural screen of the poor, and other traditional/oral people, has been reduced to "pie in the sky" and to the role of an opiate. Such a dismissal is a reductionism and a distortion of the most egregious kind, not because narcotic uses of religion never happen, but because the deeper realities of this understanding have seldom been carefully examined. The fact is, such views can fuel deep yearnings and become mandates to seek the world that is not.

In no way do I mean to trivialize the everyday socio-economic realities of traditional people. They are, in increasing numbers, being ground up in this society. At the same time Heaven can be a way to deal with it from the "aside," with "irrelevance and impertinence" in a language one can only believe.[14] It can be a powerful religious and moral objection to the world of oppression and indignity and a claim, not susceptible to the "realists," that indeed the world is not supposed to be the way it is. We have paid too much attention to the assertion of the young Marx that religion is an opiate. I remind you that he knew very little about poverty until later and he based his claims on very little "thick" description, but adopted them largely from his reading of Ludwig Feuerbach, a thinker hardly given to close knowledge of the poor and traditional/oral people, and certainly unaware that *his* views—at least those of *The Essence of Christianity*—might stand on something less than an Archimedean veranda.[15]

Traditional religious beliefs can be narcotic as can *any* belief, certainly including political ones. I have known revolutionaries who drugged themselves with political ideas that kept them anesthetized to the systemic oppressions around them and allowed them a well-heeled and propertied existence while waiting in revolutionary patience for the kairos of a conjunction of the contradictions of capitalism and the breaking point of worker commiseration. It has not occurred to enough of us that the demeaning of traditional/oral people, and the unending attempts of change agents to impose other ideologies and plans upon them, may be a large part of the problem. Moreover, there is no religious view more narcotic than supply-side economics whose policies for the poor amount, metaphorically, to feeding the horses so that the birds can eat. The difference is that this conservative ideology is, in fact, an obscene and unconscionable defense of the privileges of the rich against the poor, one nonetheless believed by many of the affluent in arrogant and sinful self-deception. I hasten to add that other moralities and theologies alien to the worlds of traditional/oral people, and framed in different contexts, are no better.

I say preach heaven and fill it with the New Testament's radical claims. Inform it with the visions of Amos and Isaiah. Claim the supernatural and name it with the name of a Merciful Righteousness that takes up the cause of the poor and those on the margins of society. Move beyond the rock-hard petrifications of Enlightenment "universal doubt" and "reason." Claim a "pattern" in life and history that is as compelling—no, more compelling—than the nihilism, the agnosticism, and the realism of modernity; beliefs known more for their certainty about what cannot be than for what is. Proclaim a God who takes care of lilies in a world where the hills sing, never forgetting that valleys rise up and so do people. Language cannot contain a Mystery that will not let this world alone, but it can, and does, point to a "pattern," to some hope born in the crushing magnitude of death that will not let us go. Language, it seems, cannot conjure a representative picture of the world as it somehow ultimately is; but testimonies, tacit and explicit, do lay claim to a reconfiguration and transformation of life in the face of the enormities of exploitation and oppression and of futility and despair.

A Word for Buford

Jimmy Hope Smith is a friend of mine who grew up in Mississippi. None of his family had ever gone to college; in fact his father never finished the sixth grade and his mother did not graduate from high school. A "strange" call to go into the ministry led him into a small liberal arts college in the South and, as he says, "infected him" with the desire to study the faith. He finished college, then seminary and went on to earn a Ph.D. at an East coast university. His family is quite proud of him, though not altogether sure about "some of his thinking."

Shortly after Jimmy Hope began teaching in a small college in the Midwest, he got a phone call from his mother in Mississippi.

"Son, you know your Uncle Buford has cancer, but it's got real bad. They say he ain't got but about six weeks to live. I want you to come down here in the next little bit and see him. I want you to talk to him, you know, to give him a word, to tell him it's gonna be all right."

Jimmy Hope's family believes that he knows some things that they don't. He went to school for so long and learned so many things that his mama knew he would know what to say, that he would be able to give Buford a word to make his dying all right.

Jimmy Hope told me that he was once talking with his father, when his dad asked him, "Son, tell me what's it like in heaven, I mean, are there really streets of gold or what?"

"Well, Daddy, I don't know, I don't have the foggiest idea."

"Then, boy, what the hell have you been doing all this time in that school up there?" was his father's unanswerable question. But his family nevertheless believes that he understands the deep mysteries of the faith and that, in a crisis like this one, Jimmy Hope would be able to bring the word. So a couple of weeks later he drove the six hundred miles to Mississippi.

Arriving late at night, he went the next morning to see his Uncle Buford. Jimmy Hope was met at the door by Buford's wife, Viola, a woman he had admired all his life. One-quarter Choctaw and three-quarters Scot, she and Buford had one of the finest marriages of love Jimmy Hope had ever known. She invited him in, hugged him, and pointed to a lounge chair in front of a TV with its back to the entry door. Jimmy Hope went around the chair and over to Buford, but was not prepared for what he found. His uncle now weighed ninety-five pounds. He looked like skin stretched over a skeleton. His eyes were enormous with pupils greatly enlarged by the morphine he took continually. When Jimmy Hope sat down, he had to make himself look at Buford, concentrating not to look away and yet to hide his shock, revulsion, and pity.

His Uncle Buford had been the blithe spirit of the family. Tall and handsome with a mane that he parted down the middle and swept back with Vaseline hair oil in the style of the day, Buford had a gait that exuded confidence. Jimmy Hope says that his Uncle Buford never walked down a street he didn't own. He did so in spite of the fact that he always struggled financially because of a basic aversion to work, on the one hand, and a life-long vocational interest in alcohol, on the other.

Buford had run away from home when he was sixteen to go to California. Jimmy Hope says that this was before the family was really sure that the roads connected Mississippi to that utopian place. From California Buford had sent pictures of himself in a white chef's outfit, complete with towel over his arm, serving soup with a ladle out of a large silver tureen. On one postcard he reported that the very night before he had actually served Clark Gable in person. The family simply nodded their heads in unison, not surprised at Buford's rising star.

Once when they had come home for a visit, Buford and Viola slept in Jimmy Hope's room. Since they always slept late, Jimmy Hope had to sneak quietly into the room to get his shoes. On the way out, he noticed that they were sound asleep, but were nevertheless snuggled up with arms around each other in a close embrace. Jimmy Hope claims that from that time on he determined that he would marry a woman who, even when he was unconscious, he would want to hold in just such a fashion. Only later did he learn that if he slept like that he woke up with both arms paralyzed from loss of circulation—a discovery that only gave him one more reason for his lionization of his Uncle Buford and the romantic mystery of his Aunt Viola.

Weak, breathless, unable to speak above a whisper, this shrivelled picture of rampaging death before him stunned Jimmy Hope with discontinuity. Inside he was reeling and hearing his mother say "give him a word" and "make it all right." Jimmy Hope knew he was in trouble.

Then, someone knocked on the door. At first Jimmy Hope was relieved by the interruption until he found out it was his mother's sister, his Aunt Zoni. While he loves her, she is, at the least, he says, the single most inappropriate human being in the world. She had overcome her twenty-five-year bout with a hyperactive alcoholism, but the years of abuse had had their effects. When she came in, she was wearing a hairnet which she had put on the last time she combed the tinted and matted mass atop her head—about three days ago. Her makeup from that same period still attended her countenance, and the toweled bathrobe she wore was held together with safety pins since the weary buttons had surrendered long ago and gone on to their reward in the landfills beneath her couches and other furniture. Under the robe was a nightie, and, though she came from all the way across town no one seemed surprised by her too-typical attire. On each hand she had taped a plastic bag filled with ointment that either a physician or some quack had prescribed for a serious skin condition, one more legacy from her past on the wild side of life.

Raspy, profane, earthy, chainsmoking, and carrying an omnipresent tepid cup of coffee in a plastic bagged hand, she came over to give her brother, Buford, a ritualized kiss. She seemed oblivious to the tragedy that hung in the room as inescapable as the smell of cancer. Hugging Jimmy Hope she gave him a wet peck and plopped down on the couch beside him.

Zoni asked Jimmy Hope a rhetorical question about his work, but went on talking without waiting for an answer. Zoni launched into a succession of three of the absolutely worst bestiality jokes Jimmy Hope had ever heard. After each joke, Zoni broke into a call-and-response litany of laugh and cough, laugh and cough, laugh and cough. When Buford chuckled quietly after each story, it was all the encouragement Zoni needed.

Jimmy Hope despaired of being able to say anything in this context that would be helpful and decided that he would just come back tomorrow. He was about to get up and excuse himself when Zoni, after finishing her last joke, changed her tone and spoke even more directly to Buford.

"Well, I gotta go, but before I do, I need to say something. Buford, there are a lot of folks telling you that you're sick, but that you're gonna be all right. I came here this morning to tell you that they are lyin' to you, boy. You are gonna die deader than a doornail. Now we're all gonna die, but you're gonna die in the next month or so. The doctors say three to six weeks. But I gotta say somethin' to you, boy. You got to believe God. Now listen to me because I know what I'm talking about. It was God that got me to quit drinking whiskey, and I have drunk this house full. [Jimmy Hope says that this is a conservative estimate.] Buford, if you believe God and you live, it's all right. And if you believe God, and you die, it's still all right. You see, Buford, it don't make a god-damn bit of difference whether you live or die. If you believe God, it's all right."

Jimmy Hope says this all happened twenty-five years ago. Buford died three weeks later. Zoni is still sober.

Notes

Chapter 1
Will Rogers, Uncle Remus, and Minnie Pearl:
Doing Ministry in a World of Stories

1. Katie G. Cannon, *Black Womanist Ethics* (Atlanta: Scholars Press, 1988), 14.

2. Chinua Achebe, *Things Fall Apart* (New York: Fawcett Press, 1959), 10.

3. Emilie M. Townes, class lecture, Saint Paul School of Theology. Also see her work on womanist issues of justice, *Womanist Justice, Womanist Hope*, ed., Susan Thistlethwaite (Atlanta: Scholars Press, 1993).

4. Steele W. Martin and Priscilla C. Martin, *Blue Collar Ministry: Problems and Opportunities for Mainline "Middle" Congregations* (New York: Alban Institute, 1989). Chapter 3 is a helpful discussion of orality among blue collar workers.

5. David Barrett reports that 29.8 percent of Christian adults and 66.7 percent of all adults in the world are not literate. See his "Status of Global Mission, 1987," *Context, International Bulletin of Missionary Research*, 11, no. 1 (1987): 25, quoted in Anthony J. Gittins, *Gifts and Strangers: Meeting the Challenge of Inculturation* (Mahwah, N.J.: Paulist Press, 1989), 83, n.14. Gittins notes that this figure depends on how one defines "literate." I obviously mean by traditional orality people who may be able to read and write but who think in proverb, story, and relationships. David J. Hesselgrave reports that less than half of the world's population can read and write, in his *Communicating Christ Cross-Culturally: An Introduction to Missionary Communication*, 2d ed. (Grand Rapids: Zondervan, 1991), 251.

6. Eric C. Lincoln and Lawrence H. Mamiya, *The Black Church*

in the African American Experience (Durham, N.C.: Duke University Press, 1990).

7. Henry H. Mitchell and Nicholas Cooper-Lewter, *Soul Theology* (Nashville: Abingdon Press, 1986), 1–13.

8. Ada Maria Isasi-Diaz and Yolando Taranzo, *Hispanic Women: Prophetic Voice in the Church* (San Francisco: Harper & Row, 1988), 16.

9. James S. Olson and Raymond Williams, *Native Americans in the Twentieth Century* (Urbana, Ill.: University of Illinois Press, 1984), 19.

10. Young-Chan Ro, "Symbol, Myth, and Ritual: The Method of the Minjung," in *Lift Every Voice: Constructing Christian Theologies from the Underside*, ed. Susan Thistlethwaite and Mary Potter Engel (San Francisco: Harper, 1990) 47–48.

11. Walter J. Ong, *Orality and Literacy* (London: Routledge, 1982), 20–77, see esp. 41.

12. Dewayne Blackwell and Bud Lee, "Friends in Low Places."Copyright ©1990 by Careers Music, Inc. (BMA/ASCAP).

13. Ray Stevens, "The Mississippi Squirrel Revival," in the album "Greatest Hits." Written by C.W. Kalb and Carlene Kalb. Copyright ©MCA Records (1984).

14. Susana Clark and Richard Leigh, "Come from the Heart." Copyright ©1989 by SBK April Music, Inc./GSC Music/Lion-Hearted Music (ASCAP).

Chapter 2
The Practices of Traditional Orality:
Doing Ministry with Traditional/Oral People

1. I am indebted to Walter J. Ong throughout this chapter for the characteristics of orality. See especially his *Orality and Literacy* (London: Routledge, 1982), 31–77; *The Presence of the Word* (Minneapolis: University of Minnesota Press, 1967); and *Interfaces of the Word* (Ithaca, N.Y.: Cornell University Press, 1977).

2. Dick Murray, *Teaching the Bible to Elementary Children*, assisted by Ruth Murry Alexander and Ellen Shepard (Nashville: Discipleship Resources, 1990).

3. Ong, *Orality and Literacy*, 9.
4. Tex Sample, *Hard Living People and Mainstream Christians* (Nashville: Abingdon Press, 1993).
5. Ong, *Orality and Literacy*, 71–74.
6. Ibid., 51.

Chapter 3
Loving Jesus and Justice:
Doing Ethics with Traditional/Oral People

1. Martin Hoffman, "The Contribution of Empathy to Justice and Moral Judgment," in *Empathy and Its Development*, ed. N. Eisenberg and J. Strayer, (New York: Cambridge University Press, 1987), 48. For a fine review of the literature see also Paul C. Vitz, "The Use of Stories in Moral Development," *American Psychologist*, 45, no. 6 (June 1990), 709–20.
2. Hoffman, "The Contribution of Empathy," 55.
3. John Milbank, *Theology and Social Theory: Beyond Secular Reason* (Cambridge: Basil Blackwell, 1990).
4. Paul C. Vitz, *American Psychologist*, 45, no. 6 (June 1990), 709–20.

Chapter 4
We Never Did It That Way Before:
Tradition, Resistance, Subversion, and Change

1. Terence Ranger, "Peasant Consciousness: Culture and Conflict in Zimbabwe," in Teodor Shanin ed., *Peasants and Peasant Societies*, 2d ed. (Oxford: Basil Blackwell Ltd., 1987), 319.
2. Walter J. Ong. *Orality and Literacy* (London: Routledge, 1982), 48.
3. Anthony Giddens, *A Contemporary Critique of Historical Materialism* (Berkeley, Calif.: University of California Press, 1981), 230–52.
4. Ranger, "Peasant Consciousness," 313.
5. James C. Scott, "Weapons of the Weak: Everyday Struggle, Meaning and Deeds," in *Peasants and Peasant Societies*, Shanin, ed., 343. For a more extended discussion see Scott's *Dom-*

ination and the Arts of Resistance: Hidden Transcripts (New Haven, Conn.: Yale University Press, 1990). For another helpful view see Michel de Certeau, *The Practice of Everyday Life*, trans. Steven Rendell (Berkeley, Calif.: University of California Press, 1984), see Introduction and 1–42.

6. Claude Levi-Strauss, *The Savage Mind* (Chicago: University of Chicago Press, 1966), 245, as quoted in Ong, *Orality and Literacy*, 39.

7. David J. Hesselgrave, *Communicating Christ Cross-Culturally: An Introduction to Missionary Communication*, 2d ed. (Grand Rapids: Zondervan, 1991).

8. Ong, *Orality and Literacy*, 37.

9. Ibid., 41f.

Chapter 5
Tradition and Practice:
Doing Indigenous Social Change

1. Karl Marx, "The Class Struggles in France, 1848 to 1850" in *Marx and Engels: Basic Writings on Politics and Philosophy*, ed. Lewis S. Feuer, (Garden City, N.Y.: Anchor Books, 1959), 314. My critique of Marx should not be misunderstood as an across-the-board dismissal of his views. There is no social theorist I appreciate more. He is a nineteenth-century thinker, but he is the most important source of ideas we have for interpreting contemporary society.

2. I am indebted to Randall Collins and Michael Makowsky, *The Discovery of Society*, 3d ed. (New York; Random House, 1984), 105–106, for this characterization of Emile Durkheim's insight, but see Durkheim's *The Elementary Forms of Religious Life*, trans. Joseph Ward Swain (New York: Collier Books, 1961), 462–96. Note, too, that one does not have to agree with Durkheim's modernist and positivist framework to find his insight helpful.

3. Anthony Gittins, *Gifts and Strangers* (Mahwah, N.J.: Paulist Press, 1989), 84–110. See also Marcel Mauss, *The Gift* (London: Cohen and West, 1970). See also the clarification of Mauss' views in Jonathan Parry, "The Gift, the Indian Gift, and

the 'Indian Gift'," *Man*, 21, no. 3 (1986), 453–73. I am indebted to Gittins for pointing out this discussion. For my earlier treatment of some of these issues in working class communities see "The Pastor as Ward Heeler," in *Blue Collar Ministry* (Valley Forge, Pa.: Judson Press, 1984), 133–48.

4. Sister Gertrude Maley, "Tell Me What They're Doing and I'll Tell You What They're Saying," unpublished paper, March, 1993. See also Gittins, *Gifts and Strangers*, 73.

5. See the helpful discussion by Hamza Alavi, "Village Factions," in *Peasants and Peasant Societies*, 2d ed., ed. Teodor Shanin (Oxford: Basil Blackwell Ltd., 1987), 346–56.

6. Ibid.

7. On this matter see Stuart Rothenberg and Frank Newport, *The Evangelical Voter* (Washington D.C.: The Institute for Government and Politics of The Free Congress Research & Education Foundation, 1984), 75–76. See also Nancy Tatom Ammerman, *Bible Believers: Fundamentalists in the Modern World* (New Brunswick, N.J.: Rutgers University Press, 1987), 188–212.

8. Tom T. Hall, "Harper Valley P.T.A." Copyright ©1967 by Newkeys Music. Copyright assigned to Unchappell Music, Inc. and Morris Music Inc.

Chapter 6
A Faith Language of the Heart:
Believing and Feeling with Traditional/Oral People

1. Quoted in James C. Edwards, *Ethics without Philosophy: Wittgenstein and the Moral Life* (Tampa: University Presses of Florida, 1982), 139. For a related discussion see Wittgenstein's *Philosophical Investigations*, trans. G. E. M. Anscombe (New York: Macmillan Publishing Co., Inc., 1958), Section 122.

2. Michael Polanyi addressed the issue of tacit knowing in his work, but his writing does not deal with the issues of class. See *Knowing and Being: Essays by Michael Polanyi*, ed. Marjorie Grene (Chicago: The University of Chicago Press, 1969), 123–37.

3. Robert J. Schreiter, *Constructing Local Theologies* (Maryknoll, N.Y.: Orbis Books, 1985), 126.

4. K. Chukwulozie Anyanwu, "Sound as Ultimate Reality

and Meaning: The Mode of Knowing Reality in African Thought,"
Ultimate Reality and Meaning, 10, 1 (March 1987): 29–38.

5. Alasdair MacIntyre, *After Virtue*, 2d ed. (Notre Dame,
Ind.: University of Notre Dame Press, 1984), 125.

6. Mary D. Pellauer and Susan Thistlethwaite, "Conversation on Grace and Healing: Perspectives from the Movement to
End Violence Against Women," in *Lift Every Voice: Constructing
Christian Theologies from the Underside*, ed. Susan Thistlethwaite
and Mary Potter Engel (San Francisco: Harper, 1990), 183–85.

7. Clifford Geertz, *The Interpretation of Cultures* (New York:
Basic Books, 1973), 3–32.

8. Henry H. Mitchell and Nicholas Cooper-Lewter, *Soul
Theology* (Nashville: Abingdon Press, 1986), 3.

9. Ibid., 6.

10. William B. McClain, "Preface," *Songs of Zion* (Nashville:
Abingdon Press, 1981), x.

11. Walter J. Ong, *Orality and Literacy*, 43–44.

12. Michel de Certeau, *The Practice of Everyday Life*, trans.
Steven Rendell (Berkeley, Calif.: University of California Press,
1984), 16.

13. José Miguez Bonino, *Toward a Christian Political Ethic*
(Philadelphia: Fortress Press, 1983), 61.

14. de Certeau, *The Practice of Everyday Life*, 16.

15. Note how Ludwig Feuerbach's view changed from *The
Essence of Christianity*, trans. George Eliot (New York: Harper
Torchbooks, 1957) to *Lectures on the Essence of Religion*, trans.
Ralph Manheim (New York: Harper & Row, 1967). See V. A.
Harvey's discussion of this change of position in "Feuerbach on
Religion as Construction," in *Theology at the End of Modernity*, ed.
S. G. Davaney (Philadelphia: Trinity Press International, 1991).

253
S1924

103634